T0246965

PRAYING
FOR
CHANGE

PRAYING
FOR
CHANGE

90
DEVOTIONS FOR
A TIME OF WAITING

VALORIE
QUESENBERRY

BARBOUR
PUBLISHING

NOBODY ENJOYS WAITING.

It's the part of life that causes us to tap a foot or doodle on a notepad or drive along the shoulder of the road in a traffic jam. We would rather do almost anything than wait.

Yet very often, God asks us to wait. In faith. In confidence. In peace. On Him. Somehow, in the divine order of things, waiting is good for our souls.

The Bible records stories of those who waited on the Lord in prayer, and it asks us to do the same. Why? Because time spent waiting is not wasted. Time spent waiting on God can be an active time for growth and flourishing. As we study the lives and prayers found in God's Word, perhaps we will ourselves be encouraged to wait in prayer, knowing that this is His way in our lives. Change is coming. And He will be good to us and redeem even the time spent in waiting as we surrender, moment by moment, to Him.

● ●

Be still and rest in the Lord; wait for Him
and patiently lean yourself upon Him.
PSALM 37:7 AMPC

REACHING FOR HOPE

*And begged Him to let them merely touch
the fringe of His garment; and as many as
touched it were perfectly restored.*
MATTHEW 14:36 AMPC

• •

We human beings need something every morning that coffee can't deliver and even a good night's sleep can't fix. We need hope. Hope from beyond ourselves and our earthly environment.

In the morning when we rise up from the forgetfulness of sleep, the problems and premonitions and paranoia from the day before come marching back into our consciousness. We feel panic building as we wonder how to handle this day on top of the concerns still unconquered from yesterday.

The only one who can help is Jesus, the healer, the hem of whose garment was full of potent glory simply from being worn by Him. The Old Testament foretold this in Malachi 4:2, referring to "healing in His wings." The word for "wings" is one used to speak of the fringes or tassels worn on the hem by Jewish men. The people of Jesus' day reached out and were restored in body and mind because of the *faith* they placed in His power. Their prayers were actual words in physical space;

ours are words ascending to His heavenly throne. But the faith is the same.

We need hope today. We can reach out to Jesus with faith and a grasp of trust.

Today. . .

- Tell God out loud what you fear and what you can't handle.

- Resolve not to turn to eating or shopping or sleeping or some other "acceptable" outlet for comfort; turn squarely to Him every time you feel panic today.

• •

Lord Jesus, when You walked the earth, Your physical presence brought calm and Your touch brought healing. Today, I come bringing with me the pain and problems of my life, and I reach out to grasp the comfort of Your presence. I wait on You today for the hope I need. Amen.

ASKING FOR MERCY

Now when the people complained, it displeased the LORD; for the LORD heard it, and His anger was aroused. So the fire of the LORD burned among them, and consumed some in the outskirts of the camp. Then the people cried out to Moses, and when Moses prayed to the LORD, the fire was quenched. So he called the name of the place Taberah, because the fire of the LORD had burned among them.

NUMBERS 11:1–3 NKJV

• •

When things are bad, we look for a rescuer. We look for someone with the knowledge and skill to make things better. A firefighter, a police officer, a doctor, a lawyer, or a pastor. We know, like the ancient Hebrews, that hope comes from getting the right resource lined up.

Many prayers of Moses are recorded in the Bible. And many of them are connected to his leadership of the people of Israel. In fact, the intercession of Moses for his people is second only to Jesus in the passion and depth of earnestness he displayed (see Exodus 32:31–32).

And here we find him yet again going to God with a plea for mercy. The people were terrible complainers, and God was angry with them. So Moses went before the Lord, and the people waited. They watched and waited with hope in the mercy of this God whom they so often disregarded. And their hope was rewarded. God caused the fire of His judgment to abate. They were saved from their punishment.

At times, people today face the judgment fire of God, though it is primarily reserved for eternity since we live in a day of grace. Sometimes, God's judgment is rendered through difficult consequences descending on us. At these times, we must wait in humility and hope.

- Cry out to God for help.
- Confess any wrongdoing.
- Cast your cares into His embrace.

• •

O God, turn aside Your judgment and give me mercy. I realize that You are my only hope. You are the resource of help I need. Where I have not done right, show me the way. Where I am prone to slip, illuminate my understanding so that I may order my day in paths of righteousness. Today, I wait on You. Amen.

TEACH US HOW

Then Manoah prayed to the LORD: "Pardon
your servant, Lord. I beg you to let the man
of God you sent to us come again to teach us
how to bring up the boy who is to be born."

JUDGES 13:8 NIV

· ·

Maybe you need instruction today. And if you do, you're not alone. Recognizing that need puts you in good company.

Instruction manuals are routinely ignored by people. The time involved in reading the instructions and the effort required to gather materials seems too large an investment of time and energy. And so the typical consumer will attempt to put together the item without the instructions.

The father and mother of Samson didn't want to risk parenting him without instructions. They prayed, imploring God to send the divine messenger back to show them how they should raise their son. They had been told that their son would take the lead in delivering Israel from her enemies. This gave them great hope for their new son. And they wanted to be sure to raise him right.

In our lives, we may know what God has promised

in His Word. We may know that He has good things ahead for us. We may have hope in His perfect plan for us. But we also need to ask for specific instruction in how to use the opportunities and gifts He has given us. Like the man Manoah and his wife, we can. . .

- Ask for wisdom.
- Offer a sacrifice to the Lord (they offered a goat for a burnt offering; we offer ourselves as a living sacrifice).

• •

Dear God, I ask for instruction in how I should use the gifts and opportunities You've given me today. Send me help in whatever way You see best. And let me be wise enough to recognize it. In Jesus' name, amen.

A COUNTENANCE
OF HOPE

Why are you cast down, O my soul? And why are
you disquieted within me? Hope in God; for I shall yet
praise Him, the help of my countenance and my God.
PSALM 42:11 NKJV

- -

If anyone knew what waiting and hoping was about, it
was King David.

Long before he was king, he was a man waiting in the
wilderness, a crowned royal in the desert, an anointed
ruler on the run. The world was a hostile place for a
shepherd boy turned king whose predecessor was not
eager to relinquish the throne. No doubt his days were
filled with confusion and doubt, with adrenaline highs
and lows, and with moments of self-doubt.

In the middle of this nomadic life, David turned
his soul toward heaven and prayed. As he waited for
God's plan to come to pass, he held on to the cord of
promise, refusing to let the chaos around him have the
final word in his commitment. He asked for a change
of countenance while he waited on God. More than a
good feeling, David desired that God's truth would even
change the way his face looked. He wanted a countenance of hope.

Perhaps you find yourself today in a cast-down situation. Maybe your hand is trembling on the cord of life. Maybe your countenance is not full of faith in the providence of our God. If so. . .

- Read Psalm 42.

- Practice a change of countenance; let your face reflect your faith.

- Tighten your grip on the cord of promise by sharing your hope with a friend.

• •

Thank You, Lord, that You are my hope and my help. As You were with David, You will be with me. Right now, I resolve to tighten my grip and deepen my trust while I wait. In Jesus' name, amen.

THE HOPE OF A FATHER

*And so, from the day we heard, we have not ceased
to pray for you, asking that you may be filled with
the knowledge of his will in all spiritual wisdom and
understanding, so as to walk in a manner worthy of
the Lord, fully pleasing to him: bearing fruit in every
good work and increasing in the knowledge of God;
being strengthened with all power, according to his
glorious might, for all endurance and patience with
joy; giving thanks to the Father, who has qualified
you to share in the inheritance of the saints in light.*

COLOSSIANS 1:9–12 ESV

• •

Parents wait for the fulfillment of prayers for their
children. Perhaps you have heard your parents pray
for you in years past. The childhood and teen years
are ones of growing, of becoming. Parents cast their
prayers upward to God and forward to the future.
Have your parents' prayers for you come to pass?
Maybe you didn't have praying parents. Sometimes,
our good Father sends others who are like parents,
who have a parental heart and will pray for us at various
seasons of our lives. These joyful friends carry us
along toward God.

The apostle Paul had a parental heart toward the

believers in Colossae. This ancient city in Asia Minor was located at the foot of a mountain and by a flowing river. It was known for a wool cloth manufactured there and dyed a purple color called *colossinus*. And there was a growing body of believers in Colossae.

As he waited for them to mature in Christ, Paul prayed for their filling, their knowledge and obedience and fruit bearing. These goals are ones we can pray for ourselves:

- Fill me with the knowledge of Your will.

- Show me how I can fully please You in my daily life.

- Strengthen me with all power so that I can endure with patience and joy and bear good fruit.

• •

O Lord, thank You for hearing my prayer based on the one for the Colossians. Help me grow more every day. In Jesus' name, amen.

ASKING IN HOPE

When he came down from the mountain,
great crowds followed him. And behold, a leper
came to him and knelt before him, saying, "Lord, if you
will, you can make me clean." And Jesus stretched
out his hand and touched him, saying, "I will;
be clean." And immediately his leprosy was cleansed.

MATTHEW 8:1–3 ESV

• •

Think about the most powerful person you know. If you had the opportunity for a personal audience, what request would you make?

This was the life Jesus lived. Everywhere He went, crowds pressed close to Him and individuals called out to Him. No one with Jesus' kind of power had ever been present in their world. And they had never seen great power coupled with great compassion. The power they knew was Rome—raw, blunt, forceful, and intimidating. Jesus, though, drew people to Himself. They really didn't understand just what kind of supernatural power was in Him, but even the little bit they saw pulled them in closer. They came in desperation, in need, in hope.

This account of a leper shows us a man who came to Jesus and made a request. The Bible usually refers to the healing of leprosy as a cleansing. This is appropriate because the disease is caused by a slow-growing bacteria. It must be cleansed out of the body. Now, we would do that with antibiotics, but this man knew nothing of that or of the microbiology of the condition. All he knew was that this man was believed to be a healer, and he recognized that as something the Messiah would do. So he asked. . .

- Humbly (he knelt, both physically and figuratively) before Jesus

- Simply (the request was easy to understand and specific)

- Hopefully ("You *can* make me clean." [emphasis added])

· ·

Savior, I acknowledge the need I have. I know You can meet it. I bow and ask You in hope today for. . . . For Christ's sake, amen.

ONLY GOD

Then Esther told them to reply to Mordecai:
"Go, gather all the Jews who are present in
Shushan, and fast for me; neither eat nor drink
for three days, night or day. My maids and I will
fast likewise. And so I will go to the king, which
is against the law; and if I perish, I perish!"

ESTHER 4:15–16 NKJV

• •

The story of Queen Esther captures the imaginations of little girls: a beautiful princess who must exercise heroic courage to speak to the king. Her immortal words recorded in scripture continue to challenge and inspire Christians today "If I perish, I perish!"

She was saying, "My life is expendable for the plan of God." She valued His people more than her life. Yet she prayed before she approached the king. She asked Mordecai and her friends to pray. She prayed for God to soften the king's heart toward her. She prayed for Him to grant her favor in a situation that was dicey and often favorless.

In our lives, we face situations that require courage. But they also demand preparation in prayer. Like Esther's circumstances, there are times when the status quo is not favorable and the winds of resistance are steady. As we turn our faces toward these assaults on our families, our morals, our freedoms, and our testimonies, may we implore the God of heaven for wisdom and for strength and for His preparatory power to soften hearts.

- Determine to value God's plan above your comfort and anonymity.

- Ask family and friends to pray with you.

- Take decisive action, expecting God to soften hearts and work on your behalf.

• •

Heavenly Father, like Esther, I lay my life before
You and ask You to intervene in this situation.
I am attempting to do something that requires
a change of heart in the other person. I ask You
to do what I cannot. In Jesus' name, amen.

PRAYER AND FASTING FOR CHANGE

And when they had come to the multitude, a man came to Him, kneeling down to Him and saying, "Lord, have mercy on my son, for he is an epileptic and suffers severely; for he often falls into the fire and often into the water." . . . So Jesus said to them, "Assuredly, I say to you, if you have faith as a mustard seed, you will say to this mountain, 'Move from here to there,' and it will move; and nothing will be impossible for you. However, this kind does not go out except by prayer and fasting."
MATTHEW 17:14–15, 20–21 NKJV

. . . .

Denying ourselves anything is difficult, isn't it? It's so much harder to say no to ourselves than to say yes. But Jesus taught His disciples that there are some kinds of change that come only through earnest petition to God. Why? No one on earth knows. But we can trust that the God who knows us intimately and who loves us unconditionally has very good reasons for everything He does in a certain way.

Prayer should be a part of everyday life. Prayer is communication with the heavenly Father. It is not to be odd or cold, awkward, or infrequent. It is an ongoing conversation with the one who loves us best, the one with whom we are in eternal relationship through the blood of Jesus Christ. If we do not stay in communication, the relationship suffers (much like earthly relationships).

Yet, sometimes, there is a need for an intentional, lengthy conversation when we are willing to sacrifice time and food and comfort for the greater good in our lives and in the lives of others. Remember. . .

- Desperate needs produce intense communication.

- Even tiny faith can move mountainous obstacles if it is centered in the person of Christ.

- Nothing is impossible if God wills it to be so.

· ·

Thank You, Father God, that You are the mountain-moving one. Give me grace to converse with You in this relationship and, if needed, to deny myself the usual daily comforts in order to discuss with You the changes I need to see in my life and in the lives of those I love. In Jesus' name, amen.

FROM COMPLAINING
TO CONFESSING

And the people spoke against God and against Moses,
Why have you brought us out of Egypt to die in the
wilderness? For there is no bread, neither is there
any water, and we loathe this light (contemptible,
unsubstantial) manna. Then the Lord sent fiery
(burning) serpents among the people; and they bit the
people, and many Israelites died. And the people came
to Moses, and said, We have sinned, for we have spoken
against the Lord and against you; pray to the Lord,
that He may take away the serpents from us. So Moses
prayed for the people. And the Lord said to Moses, Make
a fiery serpent [of bronze] and set it on a pole; and
everyone who is bitten, when he looks at it, shall live.
NUMBERS 21:5–8 AMPC

· ·

You know the symbol, right? The snake on a pole.
You've seen it on an ambulance.

People say that it stands for the staff of the ancient
Greek god of medicine. Perhaps it does. But perhaps
also it stems from this story in the Bible.

The people of Israel complained, criticizing God
and criticizing Moses. The Lord sent punishment to
them in the form of snakes with a deadly bite. God

tempers His righteous anger with times of forbearance, but this instance resulted in severe outward consequences. As a result, the people appealed to Moses. Were they truly sorry for their bitter attitudes? Only God knows. But Moses interceded. And the Lord had mercy once again on His immature and unrighteous people. Looking at the symbol of the snake on the pole would heal them.

If complaining brought about deadly snakes every time, there would be few humans left. But we look at the cross of Christ and the one who was sacrificed there to save us from the eternal death of sin. And we are changed.

- The serpent is our enemy, but Christ has crushed his head.

- The sting of sin is death, but Christ has borne it for us.

- The gift of God is eternal life.

* *

Dear Jesus, thank You for Your healing death on the cross. Looking at Your sacrifice brings about a change in us and we can live. Amen.

A HOPE WORTH
THE WAITING

*And behold, there was a man in Jerusalem whose
name was Simeon, and this man was just and devout,
waiting for the Consolation of Israel, and the Holy
Spirit was upon him. And it had been revealed to him
by the Holy Spirit that he would not see death before
he had seen the Lord's Christ. So he came by the Spirit
into the temple. And when the parents brought in the
Child Jesus, to do for Him according to the custom of
the law, he took Him up in his arms and blessed God
and said: "Lord, now You are letting Your servant
depart in peace, according to Your word; for my eyes
have seen Your salvation which You have prepared
before the face of all peoples, a light to bring revelation
to the Gentiles, and the glory of Your people Israel."*
LUKE 2:25–32 NKJV

· ·

A sale item. An amusement park ride. A buffet table. A
concert seat.

There are usually lines for these things. And eager
people wait in the lines.

The amount of time put into waiting says a great
deal about the worth of what is being waited on. Few of
us will stand in a line for something of little value. Our

time is worth more to us than the item.

Simeon was a man who had waited a long time for the Messiah. The worth of the fulfillment was of the greatest level to him. Waiting for that kind of hope was not a trial, because the anticipation of the joy made it bearable, just as Jacob was willing to wait seven years for Rachel and it seemed as nothing to him because of the love he had for her (Genesis 29:20).

The Messiah came. We now wait for His second coming. And we wait for His daily coming into the prayers we lift to Him.

- Wait in anticipation.
- Wait in hope.
- Wait in joy.

• •

O God, my heart is full, for I have seen with eyes of faith the completion of my redemption when I will stand beside You in eternal joy. Today, I lift waiting hands to You. Please be Messiah in my heart in every way. Amen.

WHEN HOPE IS DEAD

Later Elisha said, What then is to be done for her?
Gehazi answered, She has no child and her husband
is old. He said, Call her. [Gehazi] called her, and she
stood in the doorway. Elisha said, At this season
when the time comes round, you shall embrace a son.
... When Elisha arrived in the house, the child was
dead and laid upon his bed. So he went in, shut the
door on the two of them, and prayed to the Lord.

2 KINGS 4:14–16, 32–33 AMPC

• •

Death is the end of hope. The death of dreams, ambitions, careers, reputations, and relationships is tragic. But nothing is as devastating as physical death, the death of a human being. As long as there is physical life, these other things can be revived or renewed or redeemed. But when the body is dead and the soul is departed, all future hopes for earthly activity cease.

This woman had been barren, infertile, for years and miraculously conceived as a result of her generosity toward Elisha, the man of God. Now the precious son was dead. The hopes she had no doubt cherished were limp and lifeless. She ran again to the man of God.

Elisha prayed to the God of heaven, the giver of life, the restorer of hope. Elisha knew that regardless of his own actions, only God could *will* the life to return to the child. And not only can our God bring physical life, He also revives spiritual life and emotional life. He can renew broken hopes. He can reactivate severed relationships. There is an old gospel song that declares that He "swept across the broken strings, stirred the slumbering chords again."

Whatever is dead in your heart today can be restored with the breath of God. . . .

- Call it out.

- Surrender your will in the matter.

- Let others off the hook.

- Seek guidance in His Word.

· ·

Dear God, I need a change in my outlook. I bring this "dead" situation to You. Please redeem and restore it by Your power. In Christ's name, amen.

HOPE AND CONFIDENCE

*For this [very] night there stood by my side an
angel of the God to Whom I belong and Whom
I serve and worship, and he said, Do not be
frightened, Paul! It is necessary for you to stand
before Caesar; and behold, God has given you all
those who are sailing with you. So keep up your
courage, men, for I have faith (complete confidence)
in God that it will be exactly as it was told me.*

ACTS 27:23–25 AMPC

• •

Great tragedies capture our imagination. When air
travel and building construction and medical pro-
cedures go well, there is nothing to talk about; life is
routine. But when something goes awry and suffering
and destruction ensue, the human mind is fascinated,
the imagination is transfixed. And no stories are quite
as harrowing as those of peril at sea. Through the centuries, both horror and heroism have been recounted
around campfires and kitchen tables.

The apostle Paul did not lack for exciting experiences. En route to Rome, he endured the wreck of
the ship he was a prisoner in. Not all the passengers
faced this prospect calmly. Yet Paul assured them that

God had promised safety to all if they followed His instructions.

Wouldn't it be easy to endure some of our trials if we knew that everything was going to be all right? We long for reassurance as we wait for God to work in our storms. Still, God does not choose to give us this knowledge in most of our stories. Perhaps the reason He did so for Paul was to give us a glimpse into what He knows and what He can do. We may see the struggle in the water, but He sees the safety on the other side.

As we lift our prayers heavenward, we can be sure that He is firmly in control.

- Rely on the unwavering presence of God.

- Resist the temptation to default to fear.

- Recommit your life and its outcome to Him.

• •

Oh Father, I long for reassurance that I am going to be fine. Help me remember that I can have reassurance, not in words but in my faith clenching on to Your faithful character and promises. Amen.

WAITING FOR HONOR

And God listened to Leah, and she conceived and bore Jacob a fifth son. Leah said, "God has given me my wages because I gave my servant to my husband." So she called his name Issachar. And Leah conceived again, and she bore Jacob a sixth son. Then Leah said, "God has endowed me with a good endowment; now my husband will honor me, because I have borne him six sons." So she called his name Zebulun. Afterward she bore a daughter and called her name Dinah.

GENESIS 30:17–21 ESV

• •

If you've ever felt inferior to someone else's beauty and poise, then you can understand a little bit of Leah's emotional angst. Just a little. Probably none of us can fully understand what it was like for her to be pawned off on her sister's groom because she was the eldest and perhaps because she was homely and unlikely to get a husband on her own merit. Imagine the shame of being found out as an imposter bride! But there was something worse in that time than being unattractive and unattached. And that was to be childless, to be barren. Even the sound of it is like a desert. Women feared childlessness. The ability to bear many children, especially sons, was a woman's claim to respect and even to good care in her old age. It increased her husband's standing in the community and often even his appreciation for her. In this sister duel, Rachel had the beauty. . .but Leah had the babies.

Still, Leah had a secret hope. She longed for her husband's love. The only way she knew to get it was through childbirth. With every successive birth, she hoped Jacob might look at her—just once—as he did Rachel.

You have secret hopes. You long for something. You are praying earnestly. So. . .

- Realize God is just when people are not.

- Remember not to compare.

- Relinquish your will to His plan.

• •

Dear Lord, sometimes I feel unloved like Leah, but I know that I never have to earn Your favor. Yet, You do want my surrender and my trust. Help me today to put my hope in Your love and not in others'. Amen.

WAITING FOR EVERYTHING GOOD

Now may the God of peace who brought again from the dead our Lord Jesus, the great shepherd of the sheep, by the blood of the eternal covenant, equip you with everything good that you may do his will, working in us that which is pleasing in his sight, through Jesus Christ, to whom be glory forever and ever. Amen.
HEBREWS 13:20–21 ESV

• •

We tend to focus on our shortcomings. Modern religion emphasizes the great chasm between us and Jesus, rather than a thankful spirit with which to claim victory in Christ.

Yes, the span between sinful humanity and a holy God is impossible to bridge. But Jesus did it for us. And now He offers us a life of increasing growth in grace. He asks us to follow Him in obedience and surrender. He wants to equip us with everything good so that we can be pleasing in His sight.

The Pharisees of Bible times are often vilified in Sunday school lessons and sermons. For the most part, this group did have their theology wrong. They had a skewed understanding of authentic righteousness, and they had a big problem with pride. But they started out as men who wanted to please God, who wanted to get things right.

Perhaps in our zeal to correct the wrongs of the past, we today have become too focused on the other side of the equation. Some of us tend to glory in our trauma and drama and our inclination toward temptation. This is a problem too.

Praying for change in ourselves means realizing our human frailties and the strong pull of temptation but also recognizing the power of the Holy Spirit to help us resist sin and to give us the ability to please God in our daily lives.

- List your areas of weakness.

- Memorize Bible verses that speak to that temptation.

- Set your will to obey the voice of the Holy Spirit.

· ·

Dear Lord, I want to see change and victory in my personal life. Today, I commit to allowing You to equip me for every good work through Jesus. Amen.

HELP WITH IMPOSSIBLE SITUATIONS

During those many days the king of Egypt died,
and the people of Israel groaned because of their
slavery and cried out for help. Their cry for rescue
from slavery came up to God. And God heard their
groaning, and God remembered his covenant
with Abraham, with Isaac, and with Jacob. God
saw the people of Israel—and God knew.
EXODUS 2:23–25 ESV

• •

If you've ever had a job that you dreaded, you can imagine what the Israelites were feeling. Only they had no hope of quitting or putting in a résumé at a place that better suited their skills and desires. The Bible tells us in Exodus 1:14 that the Egyptian slave drivers made their lives bitter with work and that all their dealings with them were harsh and severe. There were no pleasant greetings, no consideration for sick days, no vacations, and no paycheck! It was a horrible existence.

So the people of God called out to God. They groaned to Him. They pleaded with Him for deliverance, for rescue for their sons and daughters and elderly parents.

And God heard. And answered. According to His divine schedule.

God's people didn't know what He would do or how He would do it. But they prayed, believing that this one true God they served would be able to deliver them and take care of them.

God delights in answering our prayers, but He will never sabotage His master plan by letting our human pleading decide for Him. He is open to the cry of His people, but He will not go against His own sovereign will.

Are you groaning to God for an impossible situation?

- Write down the date and the situation on a note card and keep it in your Bible so that you can rejoice when God answers.

- Look for a similar situation in the Bible and let it inspire your prayer.

- Tell a friend about your prayer and ask her to keep you accountable in your faith that God has heard and is working.

* *

O Lord, today I affirm that I trust in You and in Your perfect ways. Please hear my groaning in prayer about this circumstance and give me confidence in You. In Jesus' name, amen.

WAITING AT THE ALTAR

*Now the LORD said to Abram, "Go from your country
and your kindred and your father's house to the
land that I will show you. And I will make of you
a great nation, and I will bless you and make your
name great, so that you will be a blessing." . . . Then
the LORD appeared to Abram and said, "To your
offspring I will give this land." So he built there an
altar to the LORD, who had appeared to him. From
there he moved to the hill country on the east of
Bethel and pitched his tent, with Bethel on the west
and Ai on the east. And there he built an altar to the
LORD and called upon the name of the LORD. And
Abram journeyed on, still going toward the Negeb.*

GENESIS 12:1–2, 7–9 ESV

• •

Abram was a man who built altars. Throughout his
story in Genesis, there is a thread of seeking and sacrificing, of surrendering and sanctifying. He understood
the importance of waiting before the Lord.

The altars in Abram's life marked high points in
his relationship with his God. They were times of transition (leaving Ur), after temptation (his detour into
Egypt), during trial (waiting for the promised son), and
after testing (the call of God to sacrifice his son). During

all these times, Abram waited at an altar, bringing confession or praise, accepting the word of the Lord on the matter, and rising to follow His will.

We don't have altars of stone on mountainsides, but we have the same need to wait on God. An altar symbolized a need to reach to God. We must reach to God too. After Abram built an altar and prayed, he journeyed on. That's a good game plan for us all—build an altar and then journey on.

- Bring to God the present.

- Commit to Him the future.

- Take the next step in the journey if God does not stop you.

O Lord, I bow at the altar in my heart and ask that You would guide my heart in Your ways. Let the direction of my life be marked by Your presence. Amen.

DIRECTION FOR
THE NEXT DAY

*In these days he went out to the mountain to pray,
and all night he continued in prayer to God. And when
day came, he called his disciples and chose from them
twelve, whom he named apostles: Simon, whom he
named Peter, and Andrew his brother, and James and
John, and Philip, and Bartholomew, and Matthew,
and Thomas, and James the son of Alphaeus, and
Simon who was called the Zealot, and Judas the son
of James, and Judas Iscariot, who became a traitor.*
LUKE 6:12–16 ESV

• •

Jesus, the Son of God, waited on direction from His Father. He wanted to be perfectly in tune with the Father's will. He wanted to bring glory to His Father. Though He Himself was God, He spent time talking with His Father so that His will was perfectly aligned with the Father's, shown in these verses by His communion with Him before selecting the men who would be the twelve apostles

Getting to physical places is much simpler with the technology we have available. We don't even have to talk to a real person to find out how to get to a certain location. But getting to the spiritual destination God has for us each day is more complex. There are lessons we need to learn, truths we need to speak, souls we need to encourage, and more! Praying for the day ahead will help us stay aligned with the Father's will. It need not be a tedious part of our personal worship. Rather, slotting a few intentional minutes to be silent in His presence ensures that we are submitting our ideas to Him and letting Him speak. And even if He does not give us specifics in that morning moment, we have asked for His direction and He will guide us on the spot as we go through our day.

- Get alone with God for a few focused, quiet moments.

- Ask for His wisdom to plan and execute your day.

- Rely on the Holy Spirit "in the moment."

* *

Father God, I bring to You my day and my ideas, my responsibilities and my goals, my family and my home. Guide me today into Your divine will. Amen.

LEADING IN LOVE

*And he made his camels to kneel down outside the
city by a well of water at the time of the evening
when women go out to draw water. And he said,
O Lord, God of my master Abraham, I pray You,
cause me to meet with good success today, and show
kindness to my master Abraham. . . . The man bowed
down his head and worshiped the Lord. And said,
Blessed be the Lord, the God of my master Abraham,
Who has not left my master bereft and destitute
of His loving-kindness and steadfastness. As for
me, going on the way [of obedience and faith] the
Lord led me to the house of my master's kinsmen.*
GENESIS 24:11–12, 26–27 AMPC

• •

"Follow your heart," say Hallmark and Disney.

But the trouble with this advice, as warm and
affirming as it sounds, is that our emotions are fickle,
and our hearts are deceitful (Jeremiah 17:9). We cannot
trust our hearts, the emotional and visceral core of our
human selves, to be truthful with us or to lead us cor-
rectly. Only the Holy Spirit can do that.

Eliezer, the head servant of Abraham, understood
that he needed divine leading as he journeyed to Nahor
to find a suitable bride for Isaac, the master's son. He

did not want to rely on his own intuition or observations. He wanted the kind of success that comes from submitting plans to the Lord and letting Him guide.

The biblical record tells us that he prayed and then waited by the town well with predetermined questions that would help him know the woman God had selected. And when he knew his prayer had been answered, he praised the God of Abraham.

God is the author of human love and marriage. He has given us an instruction manual in the Bible for how to conduct our relationships. And He is the one whose direction we can seek.

- Read what the Bible says about husbands and wives and marriage.

- Ask the Holy Spirit to warn you and to show you.

- Be active in guiding your heart; don't passively let it dictate its fickle desires.

• •

Dear Lord, give me direction in affairs of the heart. I affirm that I will follow Your truth and not my undependable emotions. Amen.

UNUSUAL GUIDANCE

*There was a man in Caesarea by the name of Cornelius,
a centurion in what was called the Italian Regiment.
He was a deeply religious man who reverenced God,
as did all his household. He made many charitable
gifts to the people and was a real man of prayer.
About three o'clock one afternoon he saw perfectly
clearly in a dream an angel of God coming into his
room, approaching him, and saying, "Cornelius!"
He stared at the angel in terror, and said, "What is
it, Lord?" The angel replied, "Your prayers and your
deeds of charity have gone up to Heaven and are
remembered before God. Now send men to Joppa for
a man called Simon, who is also known as Peter." . . .
While Peter was still speaking these words the Holy
Spirit fell upon all who were listening to his message.*

ACTS 10:1–5, 44 PHILLIPS

. . . .

God often guides us in ways we don't expect. Our background or our misconceptions or even immaturity can
cause us to miss noticing what God wants us to do or
whom He wants to use.

Cornelius was a Roman soldier, a Gentile. Jews had
been commanded by God in the old covenant not to
intermarry with Gentiles or to adopt their practices

and philosophies because He knew that this would lead the people, who were without a Bible or the Holy Spirit, into confusion and error. And we see plainly that this happened many times when the Israelites disregarded His commands and descended into paganism.

But, in the new covenant, God was doing something different. The principle was the same—a holy people, separated from evil; but the application was new—the Holy Spirit was given to guide them in holiness. The apostle Peter needed to be shown this in a dramatic way, and so God gave him a vision for an illustration. While Cornelius was praying for direction, God was preparing Peter to give direction to others.

Remember. . .

- God's principles are eternally true; only the application may change.

- God's guidance always glorifies Jesus, not the person.

- God's provision results in powerful conviction.

• •

Heavenly Father, help me both to pray for direction and to be willing to give it even to those who seem unlikely if that is what You tell me to do. In Jesus' name, amen.

THE RIGHT LEADER

*Then Moses spoke to the LORD, saying: "Let the LORD,
the God of the spirits of all flesh, set a man over the
congregation, who may go out before them and go
in before them, who may lead them out and bring
them in, that the congregation of the LORD may not
be like sheep which have no shepherd." And the
LORD said to Moses: "Take Joshua the son of Nun
with you, a man in whom is the Spirit, and lay your
hand on him; set him before Eleazar the priest and
before all the congregation, and inaugurate him in
their sight."... So Moses did as the LORD commanded
him. He took Joshua and set him before Eleazar
the priest and before all the congregation. And he
laid his hands on him and inaugurated him, just
as the LORD commanded by the hand of Moses.*
NUMBERS 27:15–19, 22–23 NKJV

• •

Transition is a fearful time. When one leader steps
down, another needs to fill the vacuum. At times, the
one who assumes the role is not best suited for it. As
members of churches and associations, companies
and families, we are acquainted with all the change
such a transition brings.

Moses knew that he was old and would need a

successor. Maybe he thought about it long into the starry nights while he lay in his tent. Perhaps he mentioned it to some of his trusted men. But, regardless, he did the most important thing—he sought the help of the Lord.

We don't know how long it was before God answered him. The Bible seems to indicate that there was no delay in this instance. But there are times when God asks His people to wait for this kind of direction. When you seek the help of the Lord. . .

- Identify the need.
- Pray/request in specifics.
- Wait on the Lord.

* *

*God of heaven, when I am faced with
the responsibility of selecting leaders,
remind me that You know who is best and
help me wait on Your direction. Amen.*

ENLIGHTENING FROM THE LORD

Therefore I also, after I heard of your faith in the Lord Jesus and your love for all the saints, do not cease to give thanks for you, making mention of you in my prayers: that the God of our Lord Jesus Christ, the Father of glory, may give to you the spirit of wisdom and revelation in the knowledge of Him, the eyes of your understanding being enlightened; that you may know what is the hope of His calling, what are the riches of the glory of His inheritance in the saints, and what is the exceeding greatness of His power toward us who believe, according to the working of His mighty power which He worked in Christ when He raised Him from the dead and seated Him at His right hand in the heavenly places, far above all principality and power and might and dominion, and every name that is named, not only in this age but also in that which is to come.

EPHESIANS 1:15–21 NKJV

• •

Trade. Temples. Titles. Trinkets.

Ephesus was a city of many opportunities, but the apostle Paul prayed that the young church there would be enlightened in spiritual truth.

As we read the New Testament epistles, we don't fully know the history of the places named or completely realize the significance of the context of these divinely inspired letters. It is hard for us to imagine that these locations, which now contain crumbling ruins, were once major metropolises, prized for their culture and wealth and learning. The Ephesians were, in fact, much like us.

The apostle was writing to these believers from his prison cell in Rome, knowing that his time on earth was short. He prayed to the Lord for their continued growth in grace in Christ. They faced temptations. They encountered evil philosophies. They needed divine direction in their daily lives. And so do we:

- Eternal riches are lasting; seek them.

- Divine power comes from His strength, not ours.

- True identity is found in Christ, for all ages to come.

* *

Lord Jesus, as Paul prayed for the church at Ephesus, cause my spiritual eyes to see spiritual truths and give me direction today. Amen.

COUNSEL AND
BATTLE PLANS

*Then Jehoshaphat was afraid and set his face to seek
the Lord, and proclaimed a fast throughout all Judah.
And Judah assembled to seek help from the Lord;
from all the cities of Judah they came to seek the Lord.
And Jehoshaphat stood in the assembly of Judah and
Jerusalem, in the house of the Lord, before the new
court, and said, "O Lord, God of our fathers, are you
not God in heaven? You rule over all the kingdoms of
the nations. In your hand are power and might, so that
none is able to withstand you. . . . O our God, will you
not execute judgment on them? For we are powerless
against this great horde that is coming against us. We
do not know what to do, but our eyes are on you."*

2 Chronicles 20:3–6, 12 esv

• •

Do you feel that you are in a spiritual battle in this
season of your life? If so, you are not alone. Battles,
both physical and spiritual, have been fought by God's
people down through time. And we can rely on our God
for direction in them.

Two antagonistic nations had come together
to attack King Jehoshaphat and the people of God.
Messengers came to the palace to warn the king that

a multitude of combatants was assembling and converging on them. The Bible says that Jehoshaphat was afraid.

In our lives, we may sense that the enemy is near, ready to descend on us with temptation, with oppression, with condemnation. Our action should be the same as ancient King Jehoshaphat. We can call on the Lord for direction in how to proceed in the battle. As he said, we don't know what to do. We are powerless. But God can fight for us.

- Set your face toward God and not your fear.

- Seek wisdom from His Word.

- With your close, Christian friends or your small group, declare your dependence on Him.

* *

God of heaven, I call on You this day and ask for Your divine help in this spiritual battle. Show me how to resist Satan's advances; fight for me and give me victory. In Jesus' name I ask. Amen.

DIRECTION IN LOVE TOWARD OTHERS

Finally, brothers, pray for us, that the word of the Lord may speed ahead and be honored, as happened among you, and that we may be delivered from wicked and evil men. For not all have faith. But the Lord is faithful. He will establish you and guard you against the evil one. And we have confidence in the Lord about you, that you are doing and will do the things that we command. May the Lord direct your hearts to the love of God and to the steadfastness of Christ.

2 THESSALONIANS 3:1–5 ESV

• •

We are told to "be kind" and "let all you do be done in love." These are good admonitions if they are based in truth. Often, what the secular world calls loving someone is affirming what that person wants to do. But the Bible tells us that authentic love seeks first the glory of God and then the good of others. If it doesn't accomplish these, it is not real love.

The pathway to love for others is first having a relationship with Jesus and then daily staying close to His Word and His Spirit. Prayer is one way that we can accomplish this.

The apostle Paul prayed for the believers in the

Greek city of Thessalonica and also asked them to pray for him. He knew that only through the power of Christ could they achieve wholehearted love for God and others.

Since the fall of man and woman in the perfect garden, our enemy has tempted us to replace God's definition of love with a self-centered wish for what makes "me" happy. Realizing this, we must stay dependent on the Holy Spirit for direction in our actions toward others.

- Read His Word for spiritual understanding.

- Gather with other believers for encouragement.

- Show the compassion of Jesus but hold to truth.

* *

O Lord, give me a deep understanding of the divine kind of love You have and want to show to the world through me. Amen.

DIRECTION AGAINST THE ENEMY

Now when the Philistines heard that they had anointed David king over Israel, all the Philistines went up to search for David. And David heard of it and went down to the stronghold. The Philistines also went and deployed themselves in the Valley of Rephaim. So David inquired of the LORD, saying, "Shall I go up against the Philistines? Will You deliver them into my hand?" And the LORD said to David, "Go up, for I will doubtless deliver the Philistines into your hand."

2 SAMUEL 5:17–19 NKJV

• •

Have you found that your hardest spiritual battles sometimes follow a big event in your life? After we have experienced a joyful event or a personal victory, we are perhaps a little less guarded and a little more open to Satan's ploys.

This was certainly true for David with his lifelong enemies, the Philistines. When they heard that he had been anointed as the new king of Israel, they decided to come after him. No doubt some of them remembered his triumph over their champion, Goliath. Some of them had heard how this shepherd boy had risen to be king. And they were determined to take him down.

David did what all of us should do when faced with threats from our enemy, Satan. The Bible says he "inquired of the Lord." That can be difficult for us. We like to help God with our own ideas. To ask open-ended questions makes us feel vulnerable. And it requires faith. "What if He doesn't answer?"

David had the faith to do it. And God gave him the direction he needed.

What direction do you need today?

- Be on your guard against temptation.

- Ask God outright for direction.

- Turn your mind to trust while you wait.

• •

O Lord, You are the one who gives perfect direction. I bring to You this situation. In faith I ask, "What do You want me to do?" And I believe You are going to answer. Amen.

PRAYING FOR WISDOM IN EVERYTHING

My brethren, count it all joy when you fall into various trials, knowing that the testing of your faith produces patience. But let patience have its perfect work, that you may be perfect and complete, lacking nothing. If any of you lacks wisdom, let him ask of God, who gives to all liberally and without reproach, and it will be given to him. But let him ask in faith, with no doubting, for he who doubts is like a wave of the sea driven and tossed by the wind. For let not that man suppose that he will receive anything from the Lord; he is a double-minded man, unstable in all his ways.

JAMES 1:2–8 NKJV

• •

There are no dumb questions.

That's what our teachers told us. We have been encouraged since childhood to ask questions and to learn. But surprisingly, when it comes to spiritual matters, often we are tempted not to ask but to rely on our human wisdom.

Since this was Satan's first plan of attack with humankind and it worked so well, the suggestion to doubt God and trust ourselves is still something he uses against us. Adam and Eve gave in to bypassing

God's truth and following their own. It seemed like a good idea to them—the fruit was attractive and the thought of greater knowledge was enticing. Surely God would understand. Didn't He want them to be happy and smart?

While we can see the problem in this line of thinking from our perspective now, we are often just as foolish as they when we listen to the devil's lies. Instead, we must turn to God, the author of truth, the fount of all wisdom. He will guide us if we ask.

When you need direction, ask yourself. . .

- Does God's Word address this issue?

- Has God put a spiritual mentor in my life who can help guide me?

- Am I praying about it wanting truth or wanting permission?

• •

Heavenly Father, I trust Your Word and Your wisdom. Illuminate my understanding in situations that arise today, and let me exercise faith when I don't see. In Jesus' name, amen.

FAITH FOR A FUTURE

After these things the word of the Lord came to Abram in a vision, saying, "Do not be afraid, Abram. I am your shield, your exceedingly great reward." But Abram said, "Lord God, what will You give me, seeing I go childless, and the heir of my house is Eliezer of Damascus?" Then Abram said, "Look, You have given me no offspring; indeed one born in my house is my heir!" And behold, the word of the Lord came to him, saying, "This one shall not be your heir, but one who will come from your own body shall be your heir." Then He brought him outside and said, "Look now toward heaven, and count the stars if you are able to number them." And He said to him, "So shall your descendants be." And he believed in the Lord, and He accounted it to him for righteousness.

GENESIS 15:1–6 NKJV

• •

Abraham wanted descendants. Like all of us, he had a desire for belonging, for family. He wanted the delight of a child, of grandchildren, of family continuity. But he and his wife, Sarah, could not conceive a child together. And so he took his wish to the Lord. God established a covenant with Abraham that extends to this day through the Jewish people, the human line through which God brought Jesus to earth.

What needs do you have as you look into the future? No doubt it seemed to Abraham that he waited a long time for the fulfillment of God's promise. He was one hundred years old when Isaac was born. But God knew the right time. And He knows what He is planning for all of us. Our responsibility is to trust Him and follow what He tells us to do today.

- Look at your future from an eternal perspective: earthly life is short, and heaven is forever.

- Bring to God the thing that you need.

- Wait in faith.

• •

Lord, there is nothing too hard for You.
Like Abraham, I bring to You this need, believing
that You will supply it if You know it is best for
me. Thank You for Your perfect timing. Amen.

ANSWERS BY FAITH

And Jesus said to him, "I will come and heal him."
The centurion answered and said, "Lord, I am not
worthy that You should come under my roof. But only
speak a word, and my servant will be healed. For I also
am a man under authority, having soldiers under me.
And I say to this one, 'Go,' and he goes; and to another,
'Come,' and he comes; and to my servant, 'Do this,'
and he does it." When Jesus heard it, He marveled,
and said to those who followed, "Assuredly, I say to you,
I have not found such great faith, not even in Israel!"
MATTHEW 8:7–10 NKJV

• •

If you've ever tended to someone you loved who was very ill, you can understand the worry and concern of this Roman centurion as he asked Jesus to heal his servant. The original wording in this verse may suggest that this servant was a special attendant, an employee who meant more than the average to this man. Perhaps he was more like a family member than a servant. It is very likely that was the case since this Roman soldier took the trouble to seek a healer who was popular among the common people of the day.

Yet when Jesus said He would come to heal the one who was ill, the centurion demonstrated that he had more than curiosity about Jesus. He genuinely believed that Jesus could "speak" to the sickness from a distance and that it would obey His command. He believed that this problem was subject to the authority of Christ.

And Jesus marveled at this grasp of spiritual truth.

What in your life is subject to the authority of Jesus? Have you asked Him for healing? Consider. . .

- Family and friends who don't know Christ as Savior

- Financial needs

- Health concerns

- Emotional deficits

- Relational breakdown

* *

Lord Jesus, thank You for Your authority over every problem and situation I face. I bring my need to You today in full faith that You can say the word and change the outcome. I ask You for faith to believe that You are at work. Amen.

FAITH TO LIVE

While He spoke these things to them, behold, a ruler came and worshiped Him, saying, "My daughter has just died, but come and lay Your hand on her and she will live." So Jesus arose and followed him, and so did His disciples. . . . When Jesus came into the ruler's house, and saw the flute players and the noisy crowd wailing, He said to them, "Make room, for the girl is not dead, but sleeping." And they ridiculed Him. But when the crowd was put outside, He went in and took her by the hand, and the girl arose. And the report of this went out into all that land.
MATTHEW 9:18–19, 23–26 NKJV

• •

There are times in our lives when we need the faith to rise up from our beds, so to speak, and live.

Jairus was an official in the synagogue in Capernaum. He had a position of power. But death was one thing over which he had no jurisdiction. And so he came to the Master. News of Him was traveling through the villages. What did Jairus have to lose? He must have had some measure of faith because he said concerning his sick daughter, "Come and lay Your hands on her. . .and she will live" (Mark 5:23 NKJV).

Scripture says that Jesus got up and went with

Jairus. When they finally arrived at Jairus' house, the usual mourners were there, according to the custom of the day. Jesus spoke to them from the eternal perspective when He told them that she wasn't dead but sleeping. In the language of the Creator, death is only sleep for the body as the spirit is always alive. When He took her by the hand and spoke to her, she awakened.

Do you have the faith to believe that Christ can raise you up from what is afflicting you, from what is making you feel spiritually and emotionally dead?

- Dismiss the mourners (the pity-partyers) from your space.

- Believe that Jesus holds the power of spiritual life.

- Get up and do something in faith.

* *

Dear Lord, thank You for giving life to whatever You touch. Raise me up today to new strength and faith. In Your powerful name. Amen.

FAITH TO SEE

As Jesus passed on from there, two blind men followed
Him, shouting loudly, Have pity and mercy on us,
Son of David! When He reached the house and went
in, the blind men came to Him, and Jesus said to
them, Do you believe that I am able to do this? They
said to Him, Yes, Lord. Then He touched their eyes,
saying, According to your faith and trust and reliance
[on the power invested in Me] be it done to you.
MATTHEW 9:27–29 AMPC

• •

The body is the carriage for the soul, and so it is no
wonder that much of Jesus' ministry on earth was to
the bodies of men and women. While the body is temporary and the soul is eternal, human beings cannot
interact except through the body; and when the body
is impaired, interaction and communication are
hindered.

Leaving Jairus' house, Jesus then encountered two
blind men who followed behind Him shouting. They
even followed Him into the house where He was going!
Jesus asked them a question about their faith. When
they answered in the affirmative, Jesus did not refute
them. In fact, He said that their healing was contingent
on their faith, so it must have been valid because they

were healed of their blindness.

If today everything that you are asking in prayer would be answered in accordance with the faith you have in Him, what kind of answers would you receive?

We need faith to see Jesus as the divine Son and the answer, the door, the peace, the calm, the solution we need. These blind men, without the benefit of the complete Bible or the voice of the Holy Spirit, had the faith to believe.

- List your needs.

- Examine your heart for your faith level.

- Throw the weight of your spiritual trust into Christ.

* *

Dear Lord, You hold all power, but You have chosen to limit Your answers to me in accordance with my faith. I pray today believing that You can and will answer. Amen.

FAITH FOR CRUMBS

*And behold, a woman who was a Canaanite from that
district came out and, with a [loud, troublesomely
urgent] cry, begged, Have mercy on me, O Lord, Son of
David! My daughter is miserably and distressingly and
cruelly possessed by a demon! But He did not answer
her a word. And His disciples came and implored
Him, saying, Send her away, for she is crying out after
us. He answered, I was sent only to the lost sheep
of the house of Israel. But she came and, kneeling,
worshiped Him and kept praying, Lord, help me! And
He answered, It is not right (proper, becoming, or fair)
to take the children's bread and throw it to the little
dogs. She said, Yes, Lord, yet even the little pups (little
whelps) eat the crumbs that fall from their [young]
masters' table. Then Jesus answered her, O woman,
great is your faith! Be it done for you as you wish.
And her daughter was cured from that moment.*

MATTHEW 15:22–28 AMPC

• •

Jesus often marveled at the faith of those who came to
Him, especially if they were from pagan nations. This
is interesting since, as God, He knew their thoughts
and even what they were going to do before they did it.
It says to us that we can exercise our personal will in

ways that bring joy to His heart.

This mother was desperate to find help for her demon-possessed daughter. And the response of Jesus is a bit confusing to our twenty-first-century minds. But He does all things well, in perfect love for all. She would not have been able to see a reward for her faith if He had responded the first time. He gave her the opportunity to reach out and risk, to trust in Him. Like the woman who touched the hem of His garment, this Canaanite woman believed even a slight recognition from Him, the crumbs of His goodness, would heal her daughter.

Do you have that kind of faith? . . .

- For yourself?
- For your family?
- For your ministry to others?

• •

Jesus, give me the unflagging, indomitable faith to exercise my free will and to risk putting all my trust in You for what I need. Amen.

FAITH FOR THE FATHER'S WILL

And he withdrew from them about a stone's throw, and knelt down and prayed, saying, "Father, if you are willing, remove this cup from me. Nevertheless, not my will, but yours, be done." And there appeared to him an angel from heaven, strengthening him. And being in agony he prayed more earnestly; and his sweat became like great drops of blood falling down to the ground.

LUKE 22:41–44 ESV

• •

Jesus left us an example of how to face difficult things that we know are the will of God for us.

We will never face what He did. Never will we have to bear the legal weight of every sin ever committed by the human family since time began. Jesus was not morally guilty of any sin, but He assumed the official responsibility for the consequences of all sin. He took on Himself the shame and the condemnation associated with our rebellion, our evil deeds and attitudes. He knew this was what the Father had planned from the foundation of the world (Revelation 13:8). He grieved the cost; that was part of the plan too. And He surrendered to the divine will of the Father.

Though we will not face the same degree of pain as

did our Lord, we will at times be faced with an altar of suffering. We will, at that moment, have the choice of faith in the Father or of faith in ourselves. If we choose us, we will thwart what God is trying to do. If we choose the Father, we will be part of the plan He is working for our good and His glory.

Waiting in prayer in the garden with Jesus teaches us that good comes from suffering and glory comes from death to self.

- Acknowledge the death that must be experienced.

- Accept what you know to be His will.

- Arise to follow through to the waiting glory.

• •

Lord Jesus, give me the grace to follow You into death to self and to anything other than what the Father has planned. In Your name, amen.

FAITH THAT AFFECTS
THE HOUSEHOLD

*And at Capernaum there was an official whose son
was ill. When this man heard that Jesus had come
from Judea to Galilee, he went to him and asked him
to come down and heal his son, for he was at the point
of death. So Jesus said to him, "Unless you see signs
and wonders you will not believe." The official said to
him, "Sir, come down before my child dies." Jesus said
to him, "Go; your son will live." The man believed the
word that Jesus spoke to him and went on his way.
As he was going down, his servants met him and told
him that his son was recovering. So he asked them the
hour when he began to get better, and they said to him,
"Yesterday at the seventh hour the fever left him." The
father knew that was the hour when Jesus had said to
him, "Your son will live." And he himself believed, and
all his household. This was now the second sign that
Jesus did when he had come from Judea to Galilee.*

JOHN 4:46–54 ESV

· ·

When we have the kind of faith that believes in Christ,
the impact influences everyone who lives with us.

Again we see a parent coming to Christ for a sick
child. This is the classic prayer request for any culture

and century. Parents feel helpless in the face of severe illness and search for a source of healing. This father heard about Jesus and that He was near. And he went to ask for healing for his son. As in other instances, the faith of this man was so great that he turned on his heel when Jesus spoke and started home. Before he even reached his front door, he was met with the good news. And he and his family and his household staff believed in Jesus.

What kind of faith do you have today as you pray that will have an impact on your entire household? Consider. . .

- Faith for peaceful relationships
- Faith for fruitful ministry
- Faith for faithful lives

* *

Dear Lord, let my faith spill over and impact everyone in my house. Let me be a light to point others to Christ as I pray for change in my world. Amen.

FAITH TO REMOVE CHAINS

Now when Herod was about to bring him out, on that very night, Peter was sleeping between two soldiers, bound with two chains, and sentries before the door were guarding the prison. And behold, an angel of the Lord stood next to him, and a light shone in the cell. He struck Peter on the side and woke him, saying, "Get up quickly." And the chains fell off his hands. And the angel said to him, "Dress yourself and put on your sandals." And he did so. And he said to him, "Wrap your cloak around you and follow me." . . . He went to the house of Mary, the mother of John whose other name was Mark, where many were gathered together and were praying. . . . And when they opened, they saw him and were amazed.

ACTS 12:6–8, 12, 16 ESV

• •

Do you believe that God responds to corporate prayers? This story from the days of the early church reminds us that there is power in faith-filled praying.

Herod was on a rampage against believers in Christ. He had beheaded James and had put Peter in prison, presumably for the same sentence. The Christians gathered in one of their homes to pray. The Bible doesn't tell us if they had come together for the purpose of praying for Peter, but it's possible that this was part of the reason.

Miraculously, an angel was sent from God to release Peter and lead him out of the citadel to Mary's house, which may have been a frequent location for the church to meet. When he arrived, the believers were astonished to see him.

Perhaps there are chains binding you. Maybe not literal chains but emotional or spiritual bonds. Or perhaps someone you love is in bondage of some kind. The same God who delivered Peter sees that situation.

- Gather prayer support from other believers.

- Accept the way of escape God shows.

- Be prepared to rejoice.

• •

Oh Lord, I know that You want me to live in the freedom of truth and in obedience to Christ. I ask You to break the chains in my life today. For Jesus' sake I pray, amen.

FAITH AT MIDNIGHT

The crowd joined in attacking them, and the magistrates tore the garments off them and gave orders to beat them with rods. And when they had inflicted many blows upon them, they threw them into prison, ordering the jailer to keep them safely. Having received this order, he put them into the inner prison and fastened their feet in the stocks. About midnight Paul and Silas were praying and singing hymns to God, and the prisoners were listening to them, and suddenly there was a great earthquake, so that the foundations of the prison were shaken. And immediately all the doors were opened, and everyone's bonds were unfastened. . . . And they said, "Believe in the Lord Jesus, and you will be saved, you and your household." And they spoke the word of the Lord to him and to all who were in his house. And he took them the same hour of the night and washed their wounds; and he was baptized at once, he and all his family. Then he brought them up into his house and set food before them. And he rejoiced along with his entire household that he had believed in God.

ACTS 16:22–26, 31–34 ESV

• •

Every time we read this story, we are amazed at the faith of Paul and Silas, who encouraged themselves by praying and singing hymns while they suffered in a Roman jail. They had faith that God was at work in their situation, regardless of their condition. We don't know what they prayed or what they sang, but we do know that it was powerful.

Songs are written about this miracle, and testimonies are given about how praising causes mighty movements of the Lord. We love to hold on to this hope that even in the darkest moments, God is with us and His power can change things.

Not every midnight prayer-and-praise session will be the same, but all of them can change us if we believe in the God of Paul and Silas:

- He is present in every cell where His children are held.

- He gives the ability to sing in suffering.

- He comforts with His presence.

• •

Dear God, I want to have the perspective of Paul and Silas when I face trials. I trust in You in the midnight times to come. In Jesus' name, amen.

FAITH THAT OVERCOMES

And what more shall I say? For time would fail me to tell of Gideon, Barak, Samson, Jephthah, of David and Samuel and the prophets—who through faith conquered kingdoms, enforced justice, obtained promises, stopped the mouths of lions, quenched the power of fire, escaped the edge of the sword, were made strong out of weakness, became mighty in war, put foreign armies to flight. Women received back their dead by resurrection.
HEBREWS 11:32–35 ESV

For everyone who has been born of God overcomes the world. And this is the victory that has overcome the world—our faith.
1 JOHN 5:4 ESV

• •

In a world where evil often prevails and faith is dismissed for present pleasure, we are comforted to know that the Bible promises the victory of our faith in Christ.

Hebrews 11 recounts the deeds and rewards of those down through time who had waited on God and put their full trust in His Word. They were able to accomplish amazing things in the name of the Lord.

He received the glory from their triumphs.

Our lives are less violent, less risky, less needy than theirs. We have comforts that they did not. We have technologies and benefits that they could not have imagined. Yet we face the same kinds of temptations to trust in the present and to indulge in sinful pleasures.

We must remember that we can conquer in the same manner as they. We can call on the same powerful God. We can cast the entire weight of our faith in the name of Jehovah. Through Christ, victory is ours.

- Through faith, we can claim spiritual victory.

- By faith, we can resist earthly deception.

- In faith, we can call on Christ.

• •

Dear heavenly Father, thank You for victory through faith in Your Son, Jesus Christ. My obstacles are not the same as those in Hebrews 11, but my need for You is just as great. I put my faith in You today. Amen.

WAITING FOR MORE

"My soul magnifies the Lord, and my spirit has rejoiced in God my Savior. For He has regarded the lowly state of His maidservant; for behold, henceforth all generations will call me blessed. For He who is mighty has done great things for me, and holy is His name."

LUKE 1:46–49 NKJV

. . . .

There are times in our lives when we rejoice with incomplete joy. We gather with family and friends to celebrate a family event or a holiday or a professional achievement, and there is gladness and laughter and feasting and fun. But not everything is right yet.

It might be a medical test with pending results. It could be a family member going through relational dysfunction. It could even be simply the normal stress and strain of daily living. And while your face is smiling and your body is in the middle of the happy gathering, your mind and your soul are still waiting for the final piece to fall into place, for the final check mark in the box of completion.

Mary, the earthly mother of Jesus, must have felt a little like this as she rejoiced to God (her magnificent words are recorded for us in the Gospel of Luke). Even as she exulted in the miraculous workings of God through the divine conception of her child and the events surrounding the birth of this Son of promise, she was not experiencing complete resolution and perfect calm in her life. Surely, she knew there was more to come. As we pray to the heavenly Father. . .

- We can praise Him for what He has done.

- We can bring to Him the unanswered needs and the unruly emotions of the present.

- He, the God who became a tiny infant in a virgin's womb, can do what is impossible.

• •

God my Father, I bring praises to You today for the fulfillment of Your will in my life. I exalt Your name and Your great goodness. And, in the midst of my thankfulness, I bring to You my present needs and difficulties and battles. I rejoice because I know that You can work in them just as You have done before. I ask this in Jesus' name. Amen.

REJOICING IN PRAYER THROUGH SONG

Then sang Moses and the children of Israel this song unto the LORD, and spake, saying, I will sing unto the LORD, for he hath triumphed gloriously: the horse and his rider hath he thrown into the sea. The LORD is my strength and song, and he is become my salvation: he is my God, and I will prepare him an habitation; my father's God, and I will exalt him. The LORD is a man of war: the LORD is his name. . . . Who is like unto thee, O LORD, among the gods? who is like thee, glorious in holiness, fearful in praises, doing wonders? . . . The LORD shall reign for ever and ever. For the horse of Pharaoh went in with his chariots and with his horsemen into the sea, and the LORD brought again the waters of the sea upon them; but the children of Israel went on dry land in the midst of the sea.

EXODUS 15:1–3, 11, 18–19 KJV

• •

Some occasions call out for rejoicing in song, a real break-forth-into-music moment. You may have experienced one of them—a desired result on a medical test, that nick-of-time stop before you rear-ended the car in front of you, a loved one being clean from addiction, a deposit coming through when needed, et cetera. These moments bring first of all that wave of relief and then a giddy wash of emotion.

Moses and Miriam and all the host of Israel had to be feeling this way as they watched the towering crests of sea waves tumble down on their enemies, obliterating the threat to their safety. What a heady moment! They had waited so long, over four hundred years in captivity, to be free. Though they left Egypt days before, only now was the army gone with no ability to pursue them and take them back.

Wait on the Lord with a heart turned toward your future rejoicing.

- Praise Him for His help this far.

- Trust Him for ultimate victory.

- Anticipate the coming euphoria.

. . . .

Jehovah, You are the one who gives complete
freedom from the enemies of sin in all its forms
and in all its holds on me and my family. Today,
I look to You for victory and for coming joy. Amen.

THE FULFILLMENT OF REJOICING

Now there was one, Anna, a prophetess, the daughter of Phanuel, of the tribe of Asher. She was of a great age, and had lived with a husband seven years from her virginity; and this woman was a widow of about eighty-four years, who did not depart from the temple, but served God with fastings and prayers night and day. And coming in that instant she gave thanks to the Lord, and spoke of Him to all those who looked for redemption in Jerusalem.

LUKE 2:36–38 NKJV

• •

She had been a widow for seventy-seven years. We can assume from the biblical account that she had no children. We don't know why her husband died seven years after their wedding. We don't know much about her life. But we do read that she was faithful to the worship of Yahweh.

The original word translated as "depart" in this verse means "to revolt, to desert, or fall away." She did not "depart" from the temple. This woman who had lost so much in life refused to fall away from worshipping God and continued going to the temple to worship. She did not let the disappointments and disillusionments of life deter her from finding purpose and joy. She continued fasting and praying. She waited for the fulfillment of His promise, knowing that He is faithful.

And when Joseph and Mary entered with the baby Jesus and she heard what Simeon was saying, she "gave thanks to the Lord" and then told everyone she could about the fulfillment of redemption in this holy child.

Every adult human being has come face-to-face with life's difficult times. Like Anna, we can refuse to become bitter in the waiting.

- Believe that God is faithful.

- Keep the perspective of eternity.

- Rejoice at every reminder that He is bringing His purpose to pass.

• •

God of Abraham, thank You for bringing
Your purpose to fulfillment in the world
and in my life as I trust and surrender.
Today, I reaffirm my commitment to remain
steadfast as I wait. In Jesus' name, amen.

A GOAL IN REJOICING

*Blessed be the Lᴏʀᴅ God of our fathers, who
has put such a thing as this in the king's heart,
to beautify the house of the Lᴏʀᴅ which is in
Jerusalem, and has extended mercy to me before
the king and his counselors, and before all the
king's mighty princes. So I was encouraged, as
the hand of the Lᴏʀᴅ my God was upon me; and I
gathered leading men of Israel to go up with me.*

Eᴢʀᴀ 7:27–28 NKJV

• •

For almost fifty years, the temple of God in Jerusalem
had lain in ruins after the Babylonian destruction.
Now Ezra had the permission and authority of King
Cyrus of Persia to rebuild and restore and even refur-
nish the sacred place of worship. No wonder there was
rejoicing in his heart.

The temple was the center of the Jewish hope for
the future. It was the magnet that drew every faithful
Hebrew; it was the glue that held them together. They
could envision the coming day when they would be
gathered into the Promised Land and their freedom
would be complete, their health restored, and their
Messiah enthroned. If the temple was okay, they had
hope.

In our lives, often there is a center point, the rallying point for the family or church or community. It symbolizes the hope we have for the future. And every Christian, regardless of earthly center points, should have a heart firmly fixed on Christ. He is the center around which every other hope revolves.

We may not see our hopes realized in this world, but we can fix our hearts firmly on the next.

- Encourage yourself in the Lord while you wait; set your will.

- Speak to other Christians of the glad day coming; anticipate heaven.

- Praise the Lord both privately and publicly for His steadfast working, which will culminate in eternal fulfillment.

* *

Lord God, You are the creator and center of every good gift. I know that You will bring to pass exactly what is perfect and beautiful. I live in this light by Your grace. Amen.

GOD'S WORK AND REJOICING

As they ministered to the Lord and fasted, the Holy Spirit said, "Now separate to Me Barnabas and Saul for the work to which I have called them." Then, having fasted and prayed, and laid hands on them, they sent them away.... Now when the congregation had broken up, many of the Jews and devout proselytes followed Paul and Barnabas, who, speaking to them, persuaded them to continue in the grace of God. On the next Sabbath almost the whole city came together to hear the word of God.... And the word of the Lord was being spread throughout all the region.... And the disciples were filled with joy and with the Holy Spirit.

ACTS 13:2–3, 43–44, 49, 52 NKJV

• •

"Big picture" perspective is very important. Especially as Christ followers living for eternity, we need always to keep the long-range view in mind. Momentary setbacks and temporary obstacles are part of the journey; but for the committed believer, nothing can really take away the coming joy.

This kind of perspective was important for the early church. There were many problems for them as they worked to establish ministry and to bring the gospel to a hostile world. God commissioned them to consecrate two men, Barnabas and Saul (Paul), for special ministry and to send them out to other areas. The biblical record tells of persecution and resistance. But we also read that nearly the entire city came together to hear the Word of God and that the truth spread all around. That was certainly something to rejoice over!

As we involve ourselves and our families in ministry through our local churches, it is easy to be discouraged in the short-term frustrations and complications. But, like those stalwart first-century Christians, we need to keep the eternal view: everything done in the name of Christ counts, and there will be a time when others respond.

- Pray and fast for your ministry.

- Receive encouragement from other believers.

- Rejoice in those who respond to the Word.

O Lord, though I face discouragement in ministry, I know that sharing Your wonderful truth with a hurting and sinful world is close to Your heart. Help me be faithful. Amen.

REJOICING WITH CONTENTMENT

Your steadfast love, O LORD, extends to the heavens,
your faithfulness to the clouds. Your righteousness
is like the mountains of God; your judgments are like
the great deep; man and beast you save, O LORD. How
precious is your steadfast love, O God! The children of
mankind take refuge in the shadow of your wings. They
feast on the abundance of your house, and you give
them drink from the river of your delights. For with
you is the fountain of life; in your light do we see light.

PSALM 36:5–9 ESV

• •

When things are dismal and dim in our everyday world, we can have a deep contentment in the person and nature of our Father.

The psalmist David could identify with many of the distresses that we face. And many others! Not only did he have family problems and marriage issues and job difficulties, he was also being chased by a mentally unstable king. One of his sons murdered another, and still another son led a coup against his throne. Yes, David knew about difficult times.

But in this prayer of rejoicing, he extols the Lord for what he knows is true: the Lord's character and track record, the Lord's nature and dealings with mankind. God is the fountain of life for everyone who will receive Him.

You may be facing unimaginable circumstances today, things that were not supposed to be included in the life you plotted out. You may be walking through grief, trauma, or fear. But God is your refuge, your abundance, and your deep river of delight....

- His faithfulness reaches to the clouds and beyond.

- His righteousness is high like the mountains.

- His judgments are deep like the ocean.

Lord God, there is none like You. As I wait in prayer today, I find rest for my soul in You and contentment for my spirit in the knowledge that You control all things. Amen.

WHEN THORNS
CAUSE REJOICING

*So tremendous, however, were the revelations that
God gave me that, in order to prevent my becoming
absurdly conceited, I was given a physical handicap—
one of Satan's angels—to harass me and effectually stop
any conceit. Three times I begged the Lord for it to leave
me, but his reply has been, "My grace is enough for
you: for where there is weakness, my power is shown
the more completely." Therefore, I have cheerfully
made up my mind to be proud of my weaknesses,
because they mean a deeper experience of the power
of Christ. I can even enjoy weaknesses, suffering,
privations, persecutions and difficulties for Christ's
sake. For my very weakness makes me strong in him.*

2 CORINTHIANS 12:7–10 PHILLIPS

. . . .

It is rare to be excited about suffering. And the apostle
Paul was a human being like us. He did not run toward
pain, but he had made up his mind to enjoy the fruit
that it produced.

When things are painful—physically, emotionally,
or spiritually—we pray about them. We should. God is
our Father and cares deeply about what hurts us. Yet at
times, He knows that the pain is actually what is best

and not relief. Pain's presence can make us more like Christ than its absence can.

Paul was tremendously used of God in preaching and writing. He was a missionary and an apostle. He had actually spoken to Jesus on the road to Damascus. He believed that God was tempering any inclination to pride with this "thorn" with which he had to contend.

He prayed about it, but the answer he received was one of promised grace ("bearability"), not relief. God would enable him to endure, and the very endurance would give him the opportunity to lean harder on the power of Christ.

When we suffer and our prayers are answered differently than we expect, we find ourselves needing to be like the apostle Paul.

- Bring the pain to God.

- Accept the perspective of God.

- Access the grace of God.

Dear Father, I thank You that Your power is always greater than the pain of the moment. Grant me the grace I need to endure. In Jesus' name, amen.

REJOICING THROUGH LIFE

*O God, from my youth you have taught me, and I
still proclaim your wondrous deeds. So even to old
age and gray hairs, O God, do not forsake me, until
I proclaim your might to another generation, your
power to all those to come. Your righteousness,
O God, reaches the high heavens. You who have
done great things, O God, who is like you?*

PSALM 71:17–19 ESV

. . . .

At night, anxieties and contemplations mushroom in
our minds. The things that we can put aside during the
day when we must perform our other tasks come back
to linger as our bodies try to relax and our brains long
to rest.

Perhaps the psalmist wrote this passage in the
night hours. Maybe he deliberately turned his mind
from problems and challenges and focused on the
faithfulness and goodness of God. He looked back at
his life and proclaimed how he had been taught and
how he had been guided and helped. He remembered
great things from a great God.

When we look back at the lives we have lived, we
can see the disappointments, the battles, the sins, the
failures, the trials, the losses, the setbacks. But we can

also see a thread of grace and goodness, a golden line of divine providence woven into the fabric. From youth, we have been instructed through the Word and the Spirit. Until death, we will not be forsaken.

Perhaps the psalmist waited for morning while he wrote these words. Maybe he was waiting for better news the next day. But whatever the context, his prayer of rejoicing can be ours as we reflect on our God:

- He has mighty power for every generation.

- His righteousness is great and describes His character.

- He has done great things.

• •

Thank You, O God, that You have been loving me since I was young and will be loving me until I die. I want to live my life in Your power. I want to share in Your righteousness as long as I live. Amen.

THE FAMILY OF FAITH
AND REJOICING

Paul, messenger by God's appointment in the promised life of Christ Jesus, to Timothy, my own dearly loved son: grace, mercy and peace be to you from God the Father and Christ Jesus, our Lord. I thank the God of my forefathers, whom I serve with a clear conscience, as I remember you in my prayers. . . . I often think of that genuine faith of yours—a faith that first appeared in your grandmother Lois, then in Eunice your mother, and is now, I am convinced, in you as well. Because you have this faith, I now remind you to stir up that inner fire which God gave you at your ordination.

2 TIMOTHY 1:1–3, 5–6 PHILLIPS

· ·

The greatest community of all is the family.

God instituted the family in the very beginning. The earth was to be filled with family joy and family togetherness, family love and family support. But the first couple disobeyed their Creator, and their sin nature was passed down to their descendants. Their family produced not love and joy but hatred and anger.

Someday, God will right the wrongs in the human family; and while we wait for that day, He has given us the family of God, the body of believers in Christ. Paul prayed for young pastor Timothy, rejoicing in the biological family who had loved and trained him. Because of his mother and grandmother, Timothy possessed a genuine faith in Jehovah. Because of God's work in him, he had an inner fire that would be used for God's glory. But Paul also rejoiced in his connection to Timothy through the spiritual family.

We as Christ followers have the same family of faith, the church, with the same reasons to rejoice. . . .

- Biological families share human DNA; God's family shares divine grace.

- Human families live together on earth; God's family lives in community for eternity.

- Earthly families have shared traits; God's family shares the fire of the Spirit in their hearts.

• •

Dear God, thank You for Your family. As I wait for the perfection You will bring to humanity someday, I rejoice in the provision You have made through my second family—my brothers and sisters in Christ. Give me grace to live in love in both communities! Amen.

REJOICING IN SALVATION

You will say in that day: "I will give thanks to you,
O LORD, for though you were angry with me, your
anger turned away, that you might comfort me.
Behold, God is my salvation; I will trust, and will
not be afraid; for the LORD GOD is my strength and
my song, and he has become my salvation." With joy
you will draw water from the wells of salvation.

- -

True satisfaction is found in the depths of knowing our salvation is complete, our sins are forgiven, and our future is eternal. This knowledge produces a fount of joy like bubbling springs that keeps us settled even in difficult times.

Happiness comes and goes. The very word *happy* is based on the root word *hap*, which means "luck" or "chance" and is closely related to the words *happenstance*, *perhaps*, *hapless*, *mishap*, and *happening*. Happiness is centered in happenings and situations and circumstances; they may be good and they may be bad. They are emotionally driven.

Joy in Christ comes from our confidence in our salvation—the plan of God for redeeming us through Christ's blood and making us complete in Him. This divine work gives us a cause to rejoice because it is similar to a deep well that issues up out of the earth from underground springs. It is always flowing.

The prophet Isaiah reminds us in his prayer of rejoicing that the completion of God's work in us may take time, but we have contentment in Him all the while because the well never runs dry.

- Meditate on your salvation.

- Thank God for His plan that is being completed in your life.

- Rejoice that He is your strength and your song.

• •

O Lord, Your great salvation is a fount of never-ending satisfaction. I know that I can rejoice in You despite the happenings of life. Amen.

CREATION THEME
FOR REJOICING

And [further], You, Lord, did lay the foundation of the earth in the beginning, and the heavens are the works of Your hands. They will perish, but You remain and continue permanently; they will all grow old and wear out like a garment. Like a mantle [thrown about one's self] You will roll them up, and they will be changed and replaced by others. But You remain the same, and Your years will never end nor come to failure.

HEBREWS 1:10–12 AMPC

• •

There is a lot of fear about the earth and whether we humans can destroy our own planet. While we should be faithful stewards of what God entrusts to us, we need not wonder about the earth, because we know its founder.

We may not often think of the beginning of things, but it is an important aspect of our rejoicing. The fact that God is the source of all life and the architect of the universe should produce great joy in our minds and hearts.

The world is fallen. Humans are sinful. Nature is twisted. Weather patterns are warped. DNA is contaminated. The animal kingdom is corrupted. But the

God who created this world for good is the one who remains steadfast and sovereign over it all. He will remain permanently.

The Greek word translated as "foundation" means "to settle, to lay a basis for." Imagine that! The earth, which we know from space exploration sits at an angle on an imaginary axis, is settled on a foundation laid by the Creator. The writer of Hebrews rejoiced in the facts of creation and in the unbroken existence of the Creator.

God will one day "roll up" the heavens and replace them with a new version. But He will never change. We can pray this prayer with the Hebrew writer and find firm confidence in those facts too:

- The earth is the Lord's creation.

- The earth is secure in His hands.

- The earth will one day be changed.

Creator God, I bow before Your might and power. I rejoice in Your unending presence and Your divine plan for the universe. While I wait for Your new heaven and earth, I rejoice in knowing You personally. Amen.

THE REJOICING OF RESTORATION

*Therefore say, Thus says the Lord God: I will gather you
from the peoples. . . . They shall take away from it all
traces of its detestable things and all its abominations
(sex impurities and heathen religious practices). And
I will give them one heart [a new heart] and I will put
a new spirit within them; and I will take the stony
[unnaturally hardened] heart out of their flesh, and
will give them a heart of flesh [sensitive and responsive
to the touch of their God], that they may walk in My
statutes and keep My ordinances, and do them. And
they shall be My people, and I will be their God.*

EZEKIEL 11:17–20 AMPC

• •

Millions of dollars have been made by those who
remodel and renovate dilapidated and dated houses
into welcoming spaces.

God is in the business of renovation. His space to
work is human hearts. Since the day Adam and Eve
rebelled, His plan has been to bring us back into relationship with Him. Sin separated us. We could not have
fellowship with Him. But He promised a redeemer, a
renovator.

The story of the world told in the Bible is one in

which God was continually moving toward sinful mankind, setting the context for the Messiah. He chose the people of Abraham to be the earthly line and worked through them to that holy night in Bethlehem when Jesus was born. He continued His drawing as Jesus lived, then died and became the sacrifice that would pay the penalty for sin and bridge the gap between us and God.

In these Old Testament verses, the prophet Ezekiel wrote of the coming day when the Redeemer would give clean, soft, new hearts to those who would come to Christ for salvation. No more would they substitute the worship of self through sexual sin and pagan idolatry for the worship of Jehovah. Those who believed in Christ would walk in holy ways and be His holy people.

- Rejoice in prayer for God's work in history.
- Rejoice in prayer for God's work in our hearts.

Holy Father, thank You for a clean heart to those who come to You in repentance and faith. I rejoice today in the renovation You have done in me. Amen.

PRAYING WITH ALL THE PROMISES

For this reason I bow my knees to the Father of our Lord Jesus Christ, from whom the whole family in heaven and earth is named, that He would grant you, according to the riches of His glory, to be strengthened with might through His Spirit in the inner man, that Christ may dwell in your hearts through faith; that you, being rooted and grounded in love, may be able to comprehend with all the saints what is the width and length and depth and height—to know the love of Christ which passes knowledge; that you may be filled with all the fullness of God. Now to Him who is able to do exceedingly abundantly above all that we ask or think, according to the power that works in us, to Him be glory in the church by Christ Jesus to all generations, forever and ever. Amen.

EPHESIANS 3:14–21 NKJV

. . . .

The apostle Paul wrote often to the churches he had helped to start. These letters, or "epistles," are now part of the canon of scripture, the texts included in the Bible. Their relevance to us today is as important as back when they were written. God's words do not age; they are timeless and true.

These Jewish believers' background was one of prayers being offered by priests on holy days and of a separation from God in the temple. The Holy of Holies was not accessible to the ordinary worshipper. But when Jesus died, God ripped the curtain in the temple, symbolizing the freedom we now have through Christ to approach Him directly.

As Paul wrote to these new Christians, he told them that he bowed and prayed for them. He prayed for their growth and strength, for their rooting and grounding in Christ, for their fullness in Him. Today, we can pray the same.

- Pray for God to give you spiritual riches in Christ.

- Pray for spiritual comprehension of your standing in Christ.

- Pray for His glory to be accomplished in the church.

• •

Dear God, thank You for giving me access to Your throne through Christ. I bring to You my praise and my petitions. Help me to be rooted and grounded in Jesus. Do Your work in and through me. Amen.

THE PROMISE OF
PRAYERFUL PEACE

*Be anxious for nothing, but in everything by prayer
and supplication, with thanksgiving, let your
requests be made known to God; and the peace of
God, which surpasses all understanding, will guard
your hearts and minds through Christ Jesus.*

PHILIPPIANS 4:6–7 NKJV

• •

Perhaps no promise in scripture is claimed more often
when it comes to prayer. We are told not to be anxious
but to pray.

The apostle Paul was the human scribe for these
words, though they were divinely inspired through the
Holy Spirit. We can wonder whether he had the occasion to test out this formula in his personal life. It is
almost certain that he did. He wrote to the Corinthian
church that he was "in labors more abundant, in
stripes above measure, in prisons more frequently,
in deaths often. From the Jews five times I received
forty stripes minus one. Three times I was beaten
with rods; once I was stoned; three times I was ship-
wrecked; a night and a day I have been in the deep;
in journeys often, in perils of waters, in perils of rob-
bers, in perils of my own countrymen, in perils of the

Gentiles, in perils in the city, in perils in the wilderness, in perils in the sea, in perils among false brethren; in weariness and toil, in sleeplessness often, in hunger and thirst, in fastings often, in cold and nakedness" (2 Corinthians 11:23–27 NKJV).

Surely these situations qualify as ones that could cause anxiety. But Paul admonished his readers, then and today, to pray with promise, to rely on God's faithful declarations to guard the heart.

What needs do you have? What circumstances do you face? What thoughts clamor in your mind?

- Give thanks in prayer.

- Bring requests in prayer.

- Gain peace through prayer.

· ·

Dear heavenly Father, today I lay claim to the promise that You have given about peace through prayer. As I turn over to You my temptations to be anxious, I believe that You will keep my heart and mind through Christ. Amen.

WAITING FOR LIFE TO BEGIN

Now Isaac pleaded with the Lord for his wife, because she was barren; and the Lord granted his plea, and Rebekah his wife conceived. . . . And the Lord said to her: "Two nations are in your womb, two peoples shall be separated from your body; one people shall be stronger than the other, and the older shall serve the younger." So when her days were fulfilled for her to give birth, indeed there were twins in her womb.

GENESIS 25:21, 23–24 NKJV

• •

In biblical days, a barren woman was shamed and was suspected of some evil that had caused her infertility. She brought a reproach to her husband who then had no heirs. It was the worst fate a woman could face.

Isaac pleaded with the Lord God of heaven for his wife, Rebekah, to be able to conceive. The Bible tells us in Genesis 24:67 that Isaac loved Rebekah, so we can assume that he wanted children not only for himself but also for her sake. God answered his prayer, and she conceived not one but two babies. Twin boys struggled within her, and God told her that this would be a life-long contest between them, this vying for dominance. Yet, through this line, God would work, looking ahead to the day He planned to bring divine conception to another woman—the virgin mother of Jesus.

Prayer must give birth to life—spiritual life that only God can bring forth in us. With the saints of old, we plead with the Lord to revive us, to make us new, to give us a new beginning in Christ. And because of Calvary, it can be a reality.

- Thank God today for the plan of redemption.

- Tell someone today about new life in Him.

* *

God of life, I praise You for bringing life where there is none and for making a way for me to experience new birth in Christ. Let all my prayers be life-anticipating as I walk with You. Amen.

WAITING FOR WATER

When the water in the skin was gone, she put the child under one of the bushes. Then she went and sat down opposite him a good way off, about the distance of a bowshot, for she said, "Let me not look on the death of the child." And as she sat opposite him, she lifted up her voice and wept. And God heard the voice of the boy, and the angel of God called to Hagar from heaven and said to her, "What troubles you, Hagar? Fear not, for God has heard the voice of the boy where he is. Up! Lift up the boy, and hold him fast with your hand, for I will make him into a great nation." Then God opened her eyes, and she saw a well of water. And she went and filled the skin with water and gave the boy a drink.

GENESIS 21:15–19 ESV

• •

Hagar was a woman caught in a complex situation. A slave from Egypt, she had no rights. Her mistress, Sarah, had perfect leeway to do with her whatever she felt best served her life and her needs; and in the present situation, that meant giving Hagar to Abraham as a "vessel" to bear a child for Sarah. In that time, a child born "on the knees" of the mistress by a slave was considered her child. It was the ancient version of surrogacy, and it caused the same kinds of difficulties that it does now.

This blended family became a problem when Abraham and Sarah had their own son, Isaac. In God's plan, Hagar and her son, Ishmael, were sent away. But He had not forsaken them.

Have you felt like this mother from centuries ago? Betrayed? Used? Banished? Desperate?

- Trust in the God who gives water in barren places.

- Remember that He keeps a perfect account of the details.

- Ask Him to open your eyes to the spiritual and emotional nourishment He can provide in the desert.

• •

O Lord God, stay with me in the wilderness and help me when I am tempted to doubt. Thank You for providing for me in the lonely places. Amen.

WAITING FOR MERCY

Then the LORD said, "Because the outcry against Sodom and Gomorrah is great and their sin is very grave, I will go down to see whether they have done altogether according to the outcry that has come to me. And if not, I will know." So the men turned from there and went toward Sodom, but Abraham still stood before the LORD. Then Abraham drew near and said, "Will you indeed sweep away the righteous with the wicked? Suppose there are fifty righteous within the city. Will you then sweep away the place and not spare it for the fifty righteous who are in it? Far be it from you to do such a thing, to put the righteous to death with the wicked, so that the righteous fare as the wicked! Far be that from you! Shall not the Judge of all the earth do what is just?" . . . And the LORD went his way, when he had finished speaking to Abraham, and Abraham returned to his place.

GENESIS 18:20–25, 33 ESV

. . . .

Interceding for those who are far from God is one of the great purposes of prayer. Many times, family members pray for years for the salvation of a loved one. During that time, they come to God again and again, asking Him to spare life, to extend opportunities, and to stay

His judgment. One of the earliest examples of this kind of praying is from the life of Abraham.

The cities of Sodom and Gomorrah were evil and filled with sexual sin. Figuratively, they caused a stench to rise up to heaven. God had determined that they must be cleansed from the earth. Only holy fire can purify sin.

Abraham grieved for his foolish nephew Lot, who had chosen to live in this sinful environment. He pleaded with the Lord for Lot's life. And though God did not spare the cities, He did rescue Lot.

Perhaps you are praying for someone who needs divine rescue. If so. . .

- Ask boldly for God's intervention.
- Obey when God prompts you to spend extra time in prayer.
- Don't give up.

• •

O Lord, You are not willing that any should be lost but that all should be saved. Thank You for the prayer of Abraham, which gives me encouragement today. Amen.

WAITING FOR SONS

Then God remembered Rachel, and God listened to her and opened her womb. She conceived and bore a son and said, "God has taken away my reproach." And she called his name Joseph, saying, "May the LORD add to me another son!"

GENESIS 30:22–24 ESV

• •

Because God had promised that the Messiah would come from the human family, Jewish girls wanted to bear sons. A son was not only a woman's social security in old age; he was also the family pride—and perhaps the Promised One. Thinking about this might give us a different perspective even on the story of Jesus' birth. Did Mary want to bear the Messiah? Had she, as a devout Hebrew girl, wondered if she would be the one?

Rachel, like Sarah and Rebekah before her in the Abrahamic line, was barren. And she cried out to the Lord. Imagine her joy when she realized that she was pregnant. Did she wonder if it was a boy or a girl? No doubt. While the ancient mind knew that girls must also be born in order for the human family to continue, both fathers and mothers wanted sons—or at least more sons than daughters. A woman with many sons was respected and envied. No wonder Rachel named her firstborn Joseph, the biblical equivalent of "And I want another one please!"

Thankfully, with the full revelation of God's Word in the Bible, we value our daughters as much as our sons. Still, we wait and pray for things that we believe will make us happy and respected and honored. Only God knows if these things are within His will. But, as Rachel did, we can know where to take our requests:

- Tell God what is wrong.

- Ask Him for the solution.

- Trust His wisdom.

• •

God of Abraham, Isaac, and Jacob, waiting and praying isn't an enjoyable part of life, but it is good for me to wait and to know that You will make the best decision for me in the things I request. Help me not to doubt Your purposes and intents for me. In Jesus' name, amen.

WAITING FOR FORGIVENESS

The next day Moses said to the people, "You have sinned a great sin. And now I will go up to the LORD; perhaps I can make atonement for your sin." So Moses returned to the LORD and said, "Alas, this people has sinned a great sin. They have made for themselves gods of gold. But now, if you will forgive their sin—but if not, please blot me out of your book that you have written." But the LORD said to Moses, "Whoever has sinned against me, I will blot out of my book. But now go, lead the people to the place about which I have spoken to you; behold, my angel shall go before you. Nevertheless, in the day when I visit, I will visit their sin upon them." Then the LORD sent a plague on the people, because they made the calf, the one that Aaron made.

EXODUS 32:30–35 ESV

• •

The people God had chosen to bring the Messiah to earth had decided that they were on their own. They were tired of waiting for Moses to return from the mountain. They didn't want to worship the invisible God who had brought them out of slavery. They wanted an image they could see, a god who would let them indulge in pagan practices and let them feel good in the moment. So Aaron made a gold idol and an altar in front of it, and the people threw a big party with lots of food and sexual orgies.

This kind of sin throws its arrogance in the face of God. Moses knew that God could destroy them all. He stood before the Lord and stepped into the place of judgment with the people, asking that God blot away his name too if He would not forgive the people.

How blessed we are that even our most arrogant moments can be washed clean because of Jesus. . .and that He has the power to help us live in victory and obedience.

- Confess your sin.
- Repent and turn from it.
- Live differently by His power.

Dear Lord Jesus, thank You for making the perfect and complete atonement for my sin. Thank You for forgiveness and for power to live differently. In Your name I pray. Amen.

WAITING FOR VINDICATION

Then Samson called to the Lord and said, "O Lord God, please remember me and please strengthen me only this once, O God, that I may be avenged on the Philistines for my two eyes." And Samson grasped the two middle pillars on which the house rested, and he leaned his weight against them, his right hand on the one and his left hand on the other. And Samson said, "Let me die with the Philistines." Then he bowed with all his strength, and the house fell upon the lords and upon all the people who were in it. So the dead whom he killed at his death were more than those whom he had killed during his life.

Judges 16:28–30 ESV

. . . .

Samson's father and mother knew that their son would be special; he was to be wholly dedicated to the Lord. As a Nazirite, he would bear the reproach of having long hair as a man and would not be able to join in the Jewish rituals and festivals by drinking anything from grapevines, nor would he be allowed to mourn the deceased by coming near a dead body. All these restrictions would make him an oddball, an outcast, in Hebrew life. This set-apartness was the mark he would carry as a balance to his calling.

The story of his strength in God but his weakness for women reminds us that we cannot be too sure of ourselves. When we fool our souls into thinking we can handle anything, a fall is coming. Samson was captured and chained. He was made to work. And on the last day of his life, while the Philistines mocked and made fun of him, he prayed once more to God. He had been waiting for the right moment. Now that it had come, he knew that the only way he could accomplish the task was in the strength that would come back through God.

What strength do you need?

- Remember the source of strength— God Himself.

- Recant your own abilities.

- Rely on the one who made you.

* *

O God, You are my source of strength. You vindicated Samson, and You will also deliver me. Thank You in Jesus' name. Amen.

PRAYING AS A SERVANT

After they had eaten and drunk in Shiloh, Hannah rose. Now Eli the priest was sitting on the seat beside the doorpost of the temple of the Lord. She was deeply distressed and prayed to the Lord and wept bitterly. And she vowed a vow and said, "O Lord of hosts, if you will indeed look on the affliction of your servant and remember me and not forget your servant, but will give to your servant a son, then I will give him to the Lord all the days of his life, and no razor shall touch his head." . . . And Elkanah knew Hannah his wife, and the Lord remembered her. And in due time Hannah conceived and bore a son, and she called his name Samuel, for she said, "I have asked for him from the Lord."

1 Samuel 1:9–11, 19–20 esv

• •

Hannah saw herself as a servant and made her request to the Lord from that perspective. As a woman, she wanted to bear children. But in a greater sense, she saw herself as a servant of the Lord, surrendered to what He wanted in her life.

We aren't told how long Hannah had wanted a child or how long she had been married to Elkanah, but we do read that the household went up to Shiloh "year by year" and that "the LORD had closed her womb"(1 Samuel 1:3, 5 ESV). We don't know if she had been praying about it every year, but the waiting had been long.

She did what she knew to do. She went to the temple. She prayed to God. She vowed that she would value the child and steward him well by offering him back in the Lord's service.

There are times in our lives when we wait and wait and wait some more. God's eternal schedule is not ours. But He responds. He opened Hannah's womb. And He can open our hearts to receive what He has planned.

- Go on with your routine; Hannah did.

- Keep praying.

- Respect the spiritual leaders God allows to speak to you.

* *

Dear God, as I wait before You for my answer,
I thank You for all the blessings I now enjoy and for
the promise of Your peace in this interim. Amen.

WAITING WITH A SACRIFICE

*Then Samuel said, "Gather all Israel at Mizpah,
and I will pray to the LORD for you." . . . So Samuel
took a nursing lamb and offered it as a whole burnt
offering to the LORD. And Samuel cried out to the LORD
for Israel, and the LORD answered him. As Samuel
was offering up the burnt offering, the Philistines
drew near to attack Israel. But the LORD thundered
with a mighty sound that day against the Philistines
and threw them into confusion, and they were
defeated before Israel. And the men of Israel went
out from Mizpah and pursued the Philistines
and struck them, as far as below Beth-car.*

1 SAMUEL 7:5, 9–11 ESV

. . . .

Much of the biblical account of the nation of Israel has
to do with their turning from God, being judged by God,
and turning back to God. This usually involved them
being taken captive by other nations or fighting signif-
icant battles with other nations. The Old Testament
prophets were the spokesmen for God and played a key
role in the nation's repentance and victory in battle.

Before Jesus' atoning death on the cross, sacrifices
had to be made for sin and for petition to the Lord.
Samuel the prophet took a very young lamb to present

as a sacrifice to the Lord. The sacrificial lambs were to be the best; they had to be without blemish. Maybe they identified them ahead of time. Perhaps the children of the family all knew which lamb would be taken to the temple that year to atone for their sins. The very innocence and beauty of the lamb was to tug at the hearts of the people, to remind them of the costliness of sin.

God responded to His prophet and His people with victory. He wants to do the same for us today. We do not have to bring our own sacrifice because Jesus paid for our sins with His blood. Consider that. . .

- Sin requires a death, a blood payment.

- Old Testament sacrifices "looked ahead" to Calvary.

- Jesus' perfect sacrifice was enough for the sins of all time.

* *

*Heavenly Father, thank You for sending
Jesus to die for my sins. Amen.*

PRAYING THAT STOPS RAIN

The effective, fervent prayer of a righteous man avails much. Elijah was a man with a nature like ours, and he prayed earnestly that it would not rain; and it did not rain on the land for three years and six months. And he prayed again, and the heaven gave rain, and the earth produced its fruit.
JAMES 5:16–18 NKJV

Now Elijah the Tishbite, of Tishbe in Gilead, said to Ahab, "As the LORD, the God of Israel, lives, before whom I stand, there shall be neither dew nor rain these years, except by my word."
1 KINGS 17:1 ESV

After many days the word of the LORD came to Elijah, in the third year, saying, "Go, show yourself to Ahab, and I will send rain upon the earth."
1 KINGS 18:1 ESV

• •

Droughts are caused by weather patterns. But God controls the weather. The Old Testament account of Elijah and the withholding of rain reminds us of the power of the "effective, fervent prayer of a righteous man."

In the days before the Bible and the Holy Spirit,

when God spoke audibly to men and dealt directly in their lives through nature, people would equate the changes in weather with divine favor or judgment. This is still true in some places, especially those where witchcraft is practiced.

Since rain was needed for crops to grow and people to thrive, the stopping of rain would force the people to look for the reason and perhaps cause them to turn their hearts toward God. Even the evil king Ahab would be forced to acknowledge that God was at work.

Today, God can still work through the weather and may, at times, allow specific things to occur. But it is the praying itself that He inspired James to emphasize in his New Testament epistle. If prayer can stop rain for years, what else can it do through the power of God?

- Make a prayer list.

- Review it and ask God for direction.

- Pray through it regularly.

* *

Thank You, Lord, for the privilege of prayer and for the power it holds. Please guide me in praying for the right things and not for my own self-centered gratification. In Jesus' name, amen.

WAITING FOR FIRE
FROM HEAVEN

So Ahab sent to all the people of Israel and gathered
the prophets together at Mount Carmel. And Elijah
came near to all the people and said, "How long
will you go limping between two different opinions?
If the LORD is God, follow him; but if Baal, then follow
him." . . . Elijah the prophet came near and said,
"O LORD, God of Abraham, Isaac, and Israel, let it be
known this day that you are God in Israel, and that
I am your servant, and that I have done all these
things at your word. Answer me, O LORD, answer
me, that this people may know that you, O LORD, are
God, and that you have turned their hearts back."
Then the fire of the LORD fell and consumed the burnt
offering and the wood and the stones and the dust,
and licked up the water that was in the trench. And
when all the people saw it, they fell on their faces
and said, "The LORD, he is God; the LORD, he is God."
1 KINGS 18:20–21, 36–39 ESV

• •

God delights in answering prayers that ask large. He is
not intimidated by great human odds. He is not fearful
of defending His reputation.

Elijah the prophet knew that the people had to

make a choice. And he knew that the God of heaven was the only one who would show up in power that day.

He added to the impossibility by soaking the firewood with water and creating a trough around the altar. Then he prayed. It was a short prayer. He didn't cut himself like the false prophets or dance around in weird gyrations. He prayed, asking the one he knew for results. And God answered.

God is not stumped by your situation. Call out to Him.

- Make a choice about trust.

- Pile up your problems on an altar in your heart.

- Ask God to answer, and wait for fire.

• •

God of heaven, I am open to You this day, and I bring to You all that is in my heart. I choose You again as my God, the one I trust. In Jesus' name, amen.

PRAYING FOR BENEDICTION

Now as Solomon finished offering all this prayer and plea to the Lord, he arose from before the altar of the Lord, where he had knelt with hands outstretched toward heaven. And he stood and blessed all the assembly of Israel with a loud voice, saying, "Blessed be the Lord who has given rest to his people Israel, according to all that he promised. Not one word has failed of all his good promise, which he spoke by Moses his servant. The Lord our God be with us, as he was with our fathers. May he not leave us or forsake us, that he may incline our hearts to him, to walk in all his ways and to keep his commandments, his statutes, and his rules, which he commanded our fathers. Let these words of mine, with which I have pleaded before the Lord, be near to the Lord our God day and night, and may he maintain the cause of his servant and the cause of his people Israel, as each day requires, that all the peoples of the earth may know that the Lord is God; there is no other. Let your heart therefore be wholly true to the Lord our God, walking in his statutes and keeping his commandments, as at this day."

1 Kings 8:54–61 ESV

• •

Solomon was allowed to build the great temple to the Lord. On the day that the ark of the covenant was brought into its place in the Holy of Holies, he prayed the benedictory prayer.

On the days in our lives when God has allowed us to complete tasks in our family or ministry, we can honor His provision by offering a prayer of benediction. We can pray, as Solomon did, for His continued presence, for hearts that run toward His commandments, and for blessings that keep us near Him. This reminds everyone who hears that all good things come from Him. Consider these truths about prayer. . .

- Prayer enhances celebration.

- Prayer completes satisfaction.

- Prayer certifies conviction.

• •

Dear Lord God, there is no task that can be completed without Your help, for our very breath and strength come from Your hand. Thank You for moments of benediction and blessing. Amen.

PRAYING AND PUNISHMENT

So David said to Nathan, "I have sinned against the
LORD." And Nathan said to David, "The LORD also
has put away your sin; you shall not die. However,
because by this deed you have given great occasion
to the enemies of the LORD to blaspheme, the child
also who is born to you shall surely die." Then Nathan
departed to his house. And the LORD struck the child
that Uriah's wife bore to David, and it became ill.
David therefore pleaded with God for the child, and
David fasted and went in and lay all night on the
ground. So the elders of his house arose and went
to him, to raise him up from the ground. But he
would not, nor did he eat food with them. Then on
the seventh day it came to pass that the child died.

2 SAMUEL 12:13–18 NKJV

• •

After David committed adultery, he acknowledged and
confessed his sin. Yet God had determined that the
infant child that had been born would not live. In those
days before the full revelation of scripture, the atoning death of Jesus, and the individual guidance of the
Holy Spirit, the Lord often moved directly in people's
lives as a result of either His favor or His retribution.
There were often dreams and deaths, droughts and

deliverances. In this case, God allowed the baby to die so that King David would know that his sin was costly. Sin always brings about some form of death.

Deaths today are usually not directly tied to the sin of a family member. Often, though, we pray for a life to be spared and it is not. This does not mean that God is punishing us or the person who died. It does remind us that the fact of sin in our world brings the fallenness that leads to death. But thanks be to God that one day, death will die! And life everlasting will be here to stay.

Celebrate that. . .

- Death is our enemy.

- Jesus conquered death.

- Life will win the final battle.

• •

Lord Jesus, thank You for conquering death for me, and thank You for the hope of eternal life with You. Amen.

PRAYING FOR PARDON

Have mercy upon me, O God, according to Your lovingkindness; according to the multitude of Your tender mercies, blot out my transgressions. Wash me thoroughly from my iniquity, and cleanse me from my sin. For I acknowledge my transgressions, and my sin is always before me. Against You, You only, have I sinned, and done this evil in Your sight. . . . Create in me a clean heart, O God, and renew a steadfast spirit within me. Do not cast me away from Your presence, and do not take Your Holy Spirit from me. Restore to me the joy of Your salvation, and uphold me by Your generous Spirit. Then I will teach transgressors Your ways, and sinners shall be converted to You.

PSALM 51:1–4, 10–13 NKJV

• •

We remember the sin of King David with Bathsheba and the subsequent murder of her husband. It is a blight on his royal record and one of the facts most closely associated with him. Yet he confessed his sin and repented of his evil. He returned to the Lord and prayed a prayer of great humility and confession.

These words of David have resonated with generations of sinners who long for clean hands and clean hearts. In his expression of grief for his heinous acts,

David verbalized the heart cries of every sinner who comes before a holy God.

If you have never come to the Lord in confession and repentance for your personal sins, you can do so today with this ancient prayer of David. There is no greater peace than the kind that comes with a cleansed soul, miraculously washed by the atoning death of Jesus.

- Confess that you are a sinner.

- Turn your back on evil ways.

- Ask God for pardon.

- Believe that Jesus is the only way to heaven.

· ·

*Dear God, thank You that Jesus' shed blood
can cleanse me from every sin. I praise
You for Your gift of salvation. Amen.*

PRAYING FOR
EXTENDED LIFE

In those days Hezekiah was sick and near death.
And Isaiah the prophet, the son of Amoz, went to him
and said to him, "Thus says the LORD: 'Set your house in
order, for you shall die, and not live.'" Then he turned
his face toward the wall, and prayed to the LORD,
saying, "Remember now, O LORD, I pray, how I have
walked before You in truth and with a loyal heart, and
have done what was good in Your sight." And Hezekiah
wept bitterly. And it happened, before Isaiah had gone
out into the middle court, that the word of the LORD
came to him, saying, "Return and tell Hezekiah the
leader of My people, 'Thus says the LORD, the God of
David your father: "I have heard your prayer, I have
seen your tears; surely I will heal you. On the third
day you shall go up to the house of the LORD."'"

2 KINGS 20:1–5 NKJV

. . . .

King Hezekiah was going to die. The prophet had delivered the message. And Hezekiah turned his face to the wall and prayed.

It's unlikely you've received a direct word from the Lord predicting your death. But there may be other things in your life that seem to be resounding with the death knell. The same God who extended Hezekiah's life hears your prayers today. And the answer is in His hands.

What area of your life needs an "extension"? Do you need more grace for your relationships or for your routine? Are you struggling with your job or with your health? Is there a need in your finances or in your emotions? You can reach out to this God who said to Hezekiah, "Surely I will heal you."

This does not mean that every trial we face will be wiped away. It doesn't mean that we will not have to put in effort. But it does mean that praying always brings the resources of God's strength to us and His Spirit near to minister to us.

- Ask for His grace.

- Listen for His voice.

- Testify to His help.

• •

O God, I bring to You the needs of my life, knowing that You have the grace and strength I need. In Jesus' name, amen.

PRAYING IN PAIN

There was a man in the land of Uz, whose name was Job; and that man was blameless and upright, and one who feared God and shunned evil. . . . Then Job arose, tore his robe, and shaved his head; and he fell to the ground and worshiped. And he said: "Naked I came from my mother's womb, and naked shall I return there. The LORD gave, and the LORD has taken away; blessed be the name of the LORD." In all this Job did not sin nor charge God with wrong. . . . Then his wife said to him, "Do you still hold fast to your integrity? Curse God and die!" But he said to her, "You speak as one of the foolish women speaks. Shall we indeed accept good from God, and shall we not accept adversity?" In all this Job did not sin with his lips.

JOB 1:1, 20–22; 2:9–10 NKJV

• •

Job's life was founded on God. In the good times, he was doing what was right and avoiding what he knew to be evil. The Bible tells us that Job would offer sacrifices for his children in the event that they had sinned and he wasn't aware of it. He had a reputation as an upright man.

When the bad times came, Job grieved the same as any person. He tore his clothing and shaved his head as was the custom of the day. But he refused to blame God or charge Him with recklessness. He worshipped. This was the pattern of Job's life. In everything, he worshiped.

When his wife resorted to despair, Job did not. He realized that good and bad are in the hands of the Lord, and submission to His will was his response. He realized that in everything, God would be faithful to him.

The God who was in the whirlwinds with Job will be with us as well, as we live our lives founded on Him. . . .

- Do what is right in the easy times.

- Lay a foundation of faith.

- Accept the sovereignty of God in the hard times.

• •

O God, I ask You to increase my determination to trust You fully. Help me today to go even deeper in my foundation in You. In Jesus' name, amen.

PRAYING AND MEDITATING

The LORD will hear when I call to Him.
Be angry, and do not sin. Meditate within your
heart on your bed, and be still. Offer the sacrifices
of righteousness, and put your trust in the LORD.
There are many who say, "Who will show us any
good?" LORD, lift up the light of Your countenance
upon us. You have put gladness in my heart, more
than in the season that their grain and wine
increased. I will both lie down in peace, and sleep;
for You alone, O LORD, make me dwell in safety.
PSALM 4:3–8 NKJV

• •

Sometimes when we pray, we cannot think of something to say. Sometimes, our hearts are so full that we cannot untangle our thoughts. In these moments, we can turn to meditation.

The meditation the psalmist spoke of is a ruminating, a revolving, in the mind on the things of God. It is rehearsing memorized scripture and allowing it to speak to the soul. It is not the same as worldly meditation, which often focuses the mind on breaths or chants and lets thoughts pass without dwelling on them. It is letting the Word of God dwell in us.

David often reflected on the works of God and

anticipated His work in the future. While he waited for the kingdom and for peace and for the resolution of battle, he would encourage himself in the Lord.

Because of this, he was able to lie down and go to sleep in whatever cave or forest he happened to be hiding in. His mental state of reliance on God gave him rest. We can learn to do the same, knowing. . .

- The Lord will shine the light of His countenance on those who trust Him.

- The Lord will put gladness in the hearts of those who seek Him.

- The Lord will give rest and safety to those who delight in Him.

* *

O Lord God, I'm remembering all the good things You've done for me and thanking You for grace and strength. You are the joy of my thoughts. Amen.

PRAYER FOR
MORNING WAITING

Give ear to my words, O LORD, consider my meditation.
Give heed to the voice of my cry, my King and my God,
for to You I will pray. My voice You shall hear in the
morning, O LORD; in the morning I will direct it to You,
and I will look up. . . . But let all those rejoice who put
their trust in You; let them ever shout for joy, because
You defend them; let those also who love Your name be
joyful in You. For You, O LORD, will bless the righteous;
with favor You will surround him as with a shield.

PSALM 5:1–3, 11–12 NKJV

• •

Prayer is the very best way to start the day. When God's voice is the first one we hear, we can measure everything else by its truth. When we quiet our hearts in His presence, we will do what is right in the presence of others.

Again David verbalized the thoughts of the delighted soul, this time with a psalm that was to be set to flutes. That seems fitting for a morning song. He declared for all of us that we will direct our thoughts and petitions to heaven as we greet a new day.

There are other times of day to pray, of course. Keeping our hearts tuned to instant prayer is the attitude that every Christian should adopt. And it is not always possible to have alone time with God in the mornings. But if we can make it our practice as often as possible, we will reap the rewards in our daily lives. King David did, and so can we.

- Give thanks for a new day and new opportunities.

- Make requests for those you love.

- Ask for guidance and direction in sharing Christ's love with others.

• •

Dear Lord, the morning time is the freshest part of the day. Help me prioritize time with You whenever possible. Amen.

PRAYING IN PERIL

Then this Daniel distinguished himself above the governors and satraps, because an excellent spirit was in him; and the king gave thought to setting him over the whole realm. So the governors and satraps sought to find some charge against Daniel concerning the kingdom; but they could find no charge or fault, because he was faithful; nor was there any error or fault found in him. . . . Now when Daniel knew that the writing was signed, he went home. And in his upper room, with his windows open toward Jerusalem, he knelt down on his knees three times that day, and prayed and gave thanks before his God, as was his custom since early days.

DANIEL 6:3–4, 10 NKJV

. . . .

Prayer isn't always popular, especially when its practice labels people politically or culturally, putting a target on their backs. Praying to the God of heaven may come with persecution for those who continue. For Daniel, the stakes were even higher. His prayer time sentenced him to death row.

The Bible tells us that he had a good record of behavior and employment. He had risen above the others and was in a position of authority and trust.

Naturally, he had enemies. And they found the one portal into his life: his devotion to God.

But their plan backfired when Daniel simply carried on as usual. He went to his room and opened his window toward Jerusalem and spoke to God. They probably weren't surprised. They had suspected that he would be steadfast, and they were right. But Daniel was more afraid of being faithless than of being found out. And so he continued. How about us?

- Are you known as a person of prayer?

- Do you pray when it's inconvenient?

- Can others count on the fact that you're praying?

• •

Dear Lord of heaven, I lift my hands and heart to You as I pray for increased boldness and discipline in my prayer life. In Jesus' name, amen.

PRAYING FOR OPEN EYES

*Now the king of Syria was making war against Israel;
and he consulted with his servants, saying, "My camp
will be in such and such a place." And the man of God
sent to the king of Israel, saying, "Beware that you
do not pass this place, for the Syrians are coming
down there." Then the king of Israel sent someone to
the place of which the man of God had told him. Thus
he warned him, and he was watchful there, not just
once or twice. . . . And when the servant of the man
of God arose early and went out, there was an army,
surrounding the city with horses and chariots. And his
servant said to him, "Alas, my master! What shall we
do?" So he answered, "Do not fear, for those who are
with us are more than those who are with them." And
Elisha prayed, and said, "Lord, I pray, open his eyes
that he may see." Then the Lord opened the eyes of the
young man, and he saw. And behold, the mountain was
full of horses and chariots of fire all around Elisha.*

2 Kings 6:8–10, 15–17 NKJV

. . . .

Having heavenly vision is the way to live free of fear.

Elisha's servant had a faith problem. He couldn't
see past the obstacles so Elisha asked God to open his
eyes. Only then could he view the heavenly chariots

that were encompassing the enemy's chariots.

Sometimes, we need to pray for clearer vision. Perhaps the situation isn't as bad as we think; it's our vision that is off. God answers basic prayers that say, "Lord, help my eyes to see heavenly realities."

Are you facing an enemy army today in your classroom or office or factory? Remember that spiritual eyes see past what is obvious to what is powerful in eternal ways:

- The armies of God protect us at God's request.

- The armies of God are real even though they're of the spirit world.

- The armies of God cannot be defeated by Satan.

• •

Dear heavenly Father, thank You for the angelic guard around those who fear Your name. When I am struggling, give me eyes to see this spiritual host. In Jesus' name, amen.

PRAYING FROM THE PIT

Then Jonah prayed to the LORD his God from the fish's belly. And he said: "I cried out to the LORD because of my affliction, and He answered me. Out of the belly of Sheol I cried, and You heard my voice. For You cast me into the deep, into the heart of the seas, and the floods surrounded me; all Your billows and Your waves passed over me. Then I said, 'I have been cast out of Your sight; yet I will look again toward Your holy temple.' The waters surrounded me, even to my soul; the deep closed around me; weeds were wrapped around my head. I went down to the moorings of the mountains; the earth with its bars closed behind me forever; yet You have brought up my life from the pit, O LORD, my God."

JONAH 2:1–6 NKJV

· ·

Few of us can say we have been in a pit, but Jonah could. Was he conscious when he tumbled around in the great stomach of the sea creature? Did he know to start praying?

When we are at our lowest point, literally or figuratively, we can trust the God of heaven, who will respond to our plea. He is the one who prepares the great fish to hold rebellious prophets. He is the one who will be happiest when we come back to Him.

If he was conscious, Jonah had to have been praying. Praying for another chance. Praying for rescue. Praying that God, who could create this large creature, would also help the poor preacher who found himself inside! God will help us too. . . .

- God knows how deep He has to go with each of us in order for us to have faith.

- God knows what we will be when He has redeemed us.

• •

Dear Lord, creator God, I thank You for delivering Jonah and delivering me. Help me live in an attitude of thankfulness. Amen.

PRAYING WITH
THE PROPHET

*Though the fig tree may not blossom, nor fruit
be on the vines; though the labor of the olive may
fail, and the fields yield no food; though the flock
may be cut off from the fold, and there be no herd
in the stalls—yet I will rejoice in the LORD, I will
joy in the God of my salvation. The LORD God is
my strength; He will make my feet like deer's feet,
and He will make me walk on my high hills.*

HABAKKUK 3:17–19 NKJV

• •

As God's people, we claim the promises of the Bible
when we go through hard times. That's what godly
people have done down through time. But there are
moments when, rather than claim a promise, we have
to embrace difficult reality and choose to worship
anyway.

The prophet Habakkuk knew that there would
be times of leanness, times when there would be no
vine-dressing and no butchering. He knew that the
days would come when the gardens would not be flourishing and the families would not be feasting. And he
called the people still to rejoice and to worship.

When we pray in the middle of real distress, we are

exercising the right kind of faith. This is the determination that looks at the hard times in life and says, "*Yet I will rejoice.*"

Waiting on God in prayer is not a magic formula that turns every thorn into a candy drop. No, praying through with the prophet means that we will push through the rocks until we get to the high ground. And even if that is rough, we will keep going. All because. . .

- God gives us strength.

- God makes our spiritual footing sure and steady.

- God steadies us for the mountains.

• •

Almighty God, I am praying by faith today as I survey the rocky path before me on the way to the top. I know that I can trust You to guide me to the peak. Amen.

PRAYING BEFORE SINKING

*And in the fourth watch [between 3:00–6:00 a.m.]
of the night, Jesus came to them, walking on the sea.
And when the disciples saw Him walking on the sea,
they were terrified and said, It is a ghost! And they
screamed out with fright. But instantly He spoke to
them, saying, Take courage! I Am! Stop being afraid!
And Peter answered Him, Lord, if it is You, command
me to come to You on the water. He said, Come! So
Peter got out of the boat and walked on the water, and
he came toward Jesus. But when he perceived and felt
the strong wind, he was frightened, and as he began to
sink, he cried out, Lord, save me [from death]! Instantly
Jesus reached out His hand and caught and held him,
saying to him, O you of little faith, why did you doubt?
And when they got into the boat, the wind ceased.*

MATTHEW 14:25–32 AMPC

• •

Knowing whom to call is crucial. At pivotal moments
in our lives, we turn to the experts. We know whom
to call for medical crises, for financial woes, for legal
troubles, and on and on. With their knowledge, they
can help us in the urgent moments.

But there is no one who can help us in the supernatural except Jesus. The apostle Peter found this out in a

dramatic way when he attempted to walk to Jesus on top of the water. For a few feet, he succeeded, upheld by his faith in Jesus. But when he looked around and realized the danger, his doubt and his fear were stronger than his faith, and he began to sink. That's when he sent out his SOS prayer, "Lord, save me!"

In our lives, there will be those moments when we can't wait in prayer; it is an immediate need. Knowing that our Lord can reach out a strong hand is our reassurance when everything else is failing. So. . .

- Stay close to the Master.

- Attempt things by faith.

- Call out to Him if you need help.

Holy Lord, I praise You because I know You are trustworthy and always ready to help me when I start to sink. Amen.

POSSESSIONS THAT
TRUMP PRAYING

*And as he was setting out on his journey, a man ran up
and knelt before him and asked him, "Good Teacher,
what must I do to inherit eternal life?" And Jesus said
to him, "Why do you call me good? No one is good
except God alone. You know the commandments: 'Do
not murder, Do not commit adultery, Do not steal, Do
not bear false witness, Do not defraud, Honor your
father and mother.'" And he said to him, "Teacher, all
these I have kept from my youth." And Jesus, looking
at him, loved him, and said to him, "You lack one
thing: go, sell all that you have and give to the poor,
and you will have treasure in heaven; and come,
follow me." Disheartened by the saying, he went
away sorrowful, for he had great possessions.*

MARK 10:17–22 ESV

. . . .

The riches that are available through Jesus are spiritual. Earthly riches can be a hindrance when we pray to get closer to Jesus. They were for this young nobleman who asked Jesus how to get eternal life.

When Jesus answered, the man was taken aback. He had supposed that Christ would tell him to do some difficult thing that would involve hard work or some costly thing that would entail a large financial invest-ment. Instead, Jesus told him something that would take away every bit of earthly treasure he had. And it was too much for him. He went away still rich and, oddly, still empty.

In our lives, there are times when our prayers reveal to us an answer we don't want. In those moments, we must decide whether what we possess, either materi-ally or relationally or internally, is worth more to us than the answer we are praying for. Remember. . .

- No earthly treasure is worth eternity.

- Prayer that pauses for possessions doesn't believe in the greatness of the one prayed to.

• •

Lord, make me rely not on my stuff but on my Savior. Thank You for showing me the path of life. Amen.

PRAYING LIKE A PUBLICAN

He also told this parable to some who trusted in themselves that they were righteous, and treated others with contempt: "Two men went up into the temple to pray, one a Pharisee and the other a tax collector. The Pharisee, standing by himself, prayed thus: 'God, I thank you that I am not like other men, extortioners, unjust, adulterers, or even like this tax collector. I fast twice a week; I give tithes of all that I get.' But the tax collector, standing far off, would not even lift up his eyes to heaven, but beat his breast, saying, 'God, be merciful to me, a sinner!' I tell you, this man went down to his house justified, rather than the other. For everyone who exalts himself will be humbled, but the one who humbles himself will be exalted."

LUKE 18:9–14 ESV

• •

We call them agents today—tax agents; but in Jesus' time a publican was one who collected the people's tax for Rome. *Publican* comes from a Latin word meaning "public revenue." These men were hated by the Jews and disdained by the Romans. They had few friends and many enemies. And they were considered the worst of sinners. In that day as today, money matters were the ones that most concerned many people.

Jesus told a parable of a certain publican who prayed a righteous prayer. Immediately, He had the attention of all the Pharisees in the crowd. How could an evil man who betrayed his own people be accounted righteous?

Jesus' words told them that the man was justified because of his prayer of faith and humility and penitence, while the Pharisee relied on his own inflated sense of self-righteousness, which is worth nothing in God's eyes. God wants us to do righteous deeds but not to try to achieve goodness on our own. Because we are walking with Him. . . .

- He gives grace to humble, seeking hearts.

- He justifies those who repent, not those who preen.

- He is near to the prayer of the meek.

Father God, I know that I need Your grace every minute to live a life that pleases You. Thank You that I am justified by faith in Christ and then You enable me to bear good fruit in my life. Amen.

PRAYING FOR PENTECOST

All these with one accord were devoting
themselves to prayer, together with the women
and Mary the mother of Jesus, and his brothers
.... When the day of Pentecost arrived, they were
all together in one place. And suddenly there came
from heaven a sound like a mighty rushing wind,
and it filled the entire house where they were sitting.
And divided tongues as of fire appeared to them
and rested on each one of them. And they were all
filled with the Holy Spirit and began to speak in
other tongues as the Spirit gave them utterance.

Acts 1:14; 2:1–4 ESV

· ·

There is no substitute in the life of the believer for the power of the Holy Spirit. Jesus promised that He would send Him, and the disciples committed to praying together to be ready to receive Him.

In His physical body on earth, Jesus limited Himself to being in one place at one time. But the Holy Spirit can be in every believer's heart around the world, working, wooing, willing us along the path of godliness.

Jesus told His disciples to wait together for this "power from on high" (Luke 24:49 NKJV). And they did—praying, talking, fellowshipping, and preparing their hearts for the work He had for them. When the day finally came, they were filled to the brim with the Holy Spirit, and He gave them power for witnessing and the ability to convey their message in other languages to the many gathered in Jerusalem.

We need a fresh reliance on the indwelling fire of the Holy Spirit. We need empowerment for lives of service and witnessing. Consider this:

- The Holy Spirit comes into our hearts when we trust Christ for salvation.

- The Holy Spirit will fully control our minds and hearts as we surrender in moments of consecration.

* *

Dear Jesus, thank You for the gift of the Holy Spirit. I open my heart to receive His filling to the brim. Amen.

PRAYER FOR PURITY

For what thanksgiving can we return to God for you, for all the joy that we feel for your sake before our God, as we pray most earnestly night and day that we may see you face to face and supply what is lacking in your faith? Now may our God and Father himself, and our Lord Jesus, direct our way to you, and may the Lord make you increase and abound in love for one another and for all, as we do for you, so that he may establish your hearts blameless in holiness before our God and Father, at the coming of our Lord Jesus with all his saints.

1 THESSALONIANS 3:9–13 ESV

• •

The apostle Paul wanted the new Christians in the churches he was mentoring to grasp the meaning of living a holy life. He was praying earnestly for them that they would be awakened to this spiritual truth.

The early church was made up of growing Christians, like our churches today. They had been saved from lives of sin to serve the living God. They were baby believers who needed strength and stability. Paul knew that being established blameless in holiness before God is only possible through the power of Christ. So he was praying constantly for these Christ followers in Thessalonica.

Purity is sometimes forgotten today in our quest to be authentic and not to sound "too good." Yet the Bible tells us that God is holy, and He calls us to be as well. He is the one who establishes us, not ourselves. It is both His standard by which to live and His grace by which to do so. And one of the manifestations of this holy life is increasing in love for other believers. When we love others, we can testify that we love God with a pure heart.

- Ask God for more love for others (not a feeling but a willingness to serve and actions that seek their good).

- Ask God to establish your heart and mind in blamelessness and holiness.

* *

Dear God, Yours is the power to make me holy and to give me active love for others. I ask this today in Jesus' name. Amen.

PRAYERS FOR PEACE AND PARTNERING

To the church of the Thessalonians in God our Father
and the Lord Jesus Christ: Grace to you and peace
from God our Father and the Lord Jesus Christ....
To this end we always pray for you, that our God
may make you worthy of his calling and may fulfill
every resolve for good and every work of faith by
his power, so that the name of our Lord Jesus may
be glorified in you, and you in him, according to
the grace of our God and the Lord Jesus Christ.

2 THESSALONIANS 1:1–2, 11–12 ESV

• •

Our spiritual leaders are aware of our spiritual needs. Like the apostle Paul, they are praying for us that we will grow and surrender and excel.

Growing in grace happens as we submit ourselves to spiritual authority, as we place ourselves in environments where the Word is taught and preached, as we involve ourselves in ministry to others, and as we share our journey with other Christians who can support, rebuke, and encourage us.

God gives the gift of discernment to spiritual leaders. They can, many times, sense a need for growth in those they lead. Our pastors and group leaders and

Sunday school teachers and youth pastors may see indications that we need to grow in a certain area. And they will pray for us that God will open to us the truth we need. As we obey and surrender, we are then equipped for good works for the glory of God. Praise Him today for the fact that. . .

- God is growing us for His eternal glory.
- God is using us to help others.

• •

Dear God, as I wait in prayer for my own spiritual growth, I am thankful for those You have placed over me who pray for me and lead me closer to You. Amen.

PRAYING FOR DELIVERANCE

Hezekiah received the letter from the hand of the messengers, and read it; and Hezekiah went up to the house of the Lord, and spread it before the Lord. And Hezekiah prayed to the Lord: "O Lord of hosts, God of Israel, enthroned above the cherubim, you are the God, you alone, of all the kingdoms of the earth; you have made heaven and earth. Incline your ear, O Lord, and hear; open your eyes, O Lord, and see; and hear all the words of Sennacherib, which he has sent to mock the living God. Truly, O Lord, the kings of Assyria have laid waste all the nations and their lands, and have cast their gods into the fire. For they were no gods, but the work of men's hands, wood and stone. Therefore they were destroyed. So now, O Lord our God, save us from his hand, that all the kingdoms of the earth may know that you alone are the Lord."
ISAIAH 37:14–20 ESV

• •

Even kings need advisers, and the best kings of Israel recognized that Jehovah was their first source of wisdom. Hezekiah went to God's house and laid the messengers' letter in front of God. And he prayed.

When we have needs, do we bring them into God's presence?

It's fine to do what we know will fix the problem. If we are out of gasoline, we need to fill the tank. If the electricity has gone off, we need to flip the breaker. If we have no clean clothes, we need to wash the laundry. We don't ask God for wisdom about things He has already put into our hands. But we do need to remember that it is good and acceptable and even preferred to ask His advice before running to everyone else. Our first thought should be to lift the problem up to heaven, remembering. . .

- God is the only one who holds eternal wisdom.

- God will incline His ear to us when we call.

Almighty God, I praise Your name today. Like Hezekiah, I want to rely on Your wisdom when I am baffled and anxious. In Jesus' name, amen.

PRAYING FOR
BIGGER BORDERS

*Jabez was more honorable than his brothers; and
his mother called his name Jabez, saying, "Because I
bore him in pain." Jabez called upon the God of Israel,
saying, "Oh that you would bless me and enlarge my
border, and that your hand might be with me, and
that you would keep me from harm so that it might
not bring me pain!" And God granted what he asked.*
1 CHRONICLES 4:9–10 ESV

* *

The remarkable thing about the prayer of Jabez is that
scripture records that God granted what he asked, all
of it. This is a model that many people would like to
claim as their own.

Jabez didn't have an auspicious beginning. Even
his name, which sounds like the Hebrew word for
"pain," was a little strange. One has to wonder if his
birth was more painful than that of his brothers. Or if
his mother couldn't think of another name she liked
and so decided to link his name with the trauma of his
birth. At any rate, he was associated with pain.

But sometime in his average life, he grasped hold
of the idea of living a life pleasing to God. He was an
honorable man, and he called out to the Lord with a

specific request for blessing and borders and the benefits of God's presence and protection.

It feels self-absorbed to us to ask God for personal blessing. It seems appropriate to request this for others but not for ourselves. However, the account of Jabez tells us differently. It's okay to request blessing from God; that is only what He wants to give us anyway. And as we are blessed and reach out to pass the blessing on to others, the Christian community receives the benefits of what we have received.

- Pray for God to give you larger boundaries in which to work for His glory.

- Pray for grace to endure and for blessing as He sees fit.

• •

O Lord God, You hold the key to all things.
I pray with Jabez that You would deal
graciously and generously with me so that I
may grow in You and bless others. Amen.

PRAYING FOR
ONE ANOTHER

Walk in wisdom toward those who are outside,
redeeming the time. Let your speech always be with
grace, seasoned with salt, that you may know how you
ought to answer each one.... Epaphras, who is one
of you, a bondservant of Christ, greets you, always
laboring fervently for you in prayers, that you may
stand perfect and complete in all the will of God. For I
bear him witness that he has a great zeal for you, and
those who are in Laodicea, and those in Hierapolis.

COLOSSIANS 4:5–6, 12–13 NKJV

• •

As believers in Christ, we are part of a community of
faith that supports each other in prayer.

The apostle Paul frequently mentioned those
who ministered with him and the contributions they
were making to the ministry of the gospel. Epaphras
is named here as a faithful minister and one who fervently prayed for the church at Colossae. This is a
great reputation. As Paul, divinely inspired by the Holy
Spirit, wrote to them of the things they needed to grow
in, they had the reassurance that Epaphras was also
praying for them in this maturing process.

As we interact in our local churches, we often

see things in other believers that puzzle us and even offend us. Others are learning to follow Christ and are being shown new things by His Spirit too. And, as it is with human babies, no rate of growth is the same. We cannot assume that we know what God is teaching someone else. Waiting before the Lord in prayer for our brothers and sisters in Christ will give us hearts of compassion and a greater love for them.

- Pray that believers will stand perfect and complete in all the will of God.

- Pray that believers will walk in wisdom and grow in grace.

Dear Lord, thank You for providing for our growth as believers. Give me the spiritual understanding I need to pray for my brothers and sisters who share this family with me. Amen.

PRAYING FOR A SISTER

Then there was a woman in Joppa, a disciple called Tabitha, whose name in Greek was Dorcas (meaning Gazelle). She was a woman whose whole life was full of good and kindly actions, but in those days she became seriously ill and died. So when they had washed her body they laid her in an upper room. Now Lydda is quite near Joppa, and when the disciples heard that Peter was in Lydda, they sent two men to him and begged him, "Please come to us without delay." Peter got up and went back with them, and when he arrived in Joppa they took him to the room upstairs. All the widows stood around him with tears in their eyes, holding out for him to see dresses and cloaks which Dorcas used to make for them while she was with them. But Peter put them all outside the room and knelt down and prayed. Then he turned to the body and said, "Tabitha, get up!" She opened her eyes, and as soon as she saw Peter she sat up. He took her by the hand, helped her to her feet, and then called out to the believers and widows and presented her to them alive. This became known throughout the whole of Joppa and many believed in the Lord.

ACTS 9:36–42 PHILLIPS

• •

Tabitha (or Dorcas, as she was called in Greek) was

perhaps what we could call a Christian social worker. She loved people and ministered to them regularly.

There are those people in our local congregations of believers who lead the way in serving others. They are the ones driving the buses, organizing the dinners, teaching the classes, and on and on. They are a blessing to us. That is how the early church felt about Dorcas.

Peter's prayer for this beloved woman was powerful because God had ordained that she should be raised to life. And He will use our prayers for one another in the way that He intends.

- Pray for strength and stamina for those who work in the church.

- Pray for the specific needs of their families and lives.

· ·

Lord Jesus, help me this day to wait in prayer for those who work so diligently in my church. Bless them today. In Jesus' name, amen.

A POUTING PRAYER

The word reached the king of Nineveh, and he arose from his throne, removed his robe, covered himself with sackcloth, and sat in ashes. And he issued a proclamation and published through Nineveh, "...Who knows? God may turn and relent and turn from his fierce anger, so that we may not perish." When God saw what they did, how they turned from their evil way, God relented of the disaster that he had said he would do to them, and he did not do it.... But it displeased Jonah exceedingly, and he was angry. And he prayed to the LORD and said, "O LORD, is not this what I said when I was yet in my country? That is why I made haste to flee to Tarshish; for I knew that you are a gracious God and merciful, slow to anger and abounding in steadfast love, and relenting from disaster. Therefore now, O LORD, please take my life from me, for it is better for me to die than to live."

JONAH 3:6–7, 9–10; 4:1–3 ESV

· ·

Have you ever pouted to God?

It is true that prayer is the best place to take our raw emotions. But it is also true that we need to let Him change us in those moments through the power of His Holy Spirit.

Jonah had endured some crazy things, and yet he was still centered on himself. Now that he had preached to the people of Nineveh about the coming judgment, he wanted to see it happen. But God always responds to repentance.

As we come before God with our wayward emotions, we can place full confidence in His ability to change our hearts, knowing. . .

- He wants us to bring our temptations to Him.

- He will give us the power to act on principle and not on feeling.

. . . .

Heavenly Father, change my attitudes and give me power to act on what I know is right, disregarding the temptation to rest on my emotions. In Jesus' name. Amen.

A PROPHETIC PRAYER

My God, my God, why have you forsaken me?
Why are you so far from saving me, from the words
of my groaning? O my God, I cry by day, but you
do not answer, and by night, but I find no rest. Yet
you are holy, enthroned on the praises of Israel.
In you our fathers trusted; they trusted, and you
delivered them. To you they cried and were rescued;
in you they trusted and were not put to shame.

PSALM 22:1–5 ESV

. . . .

Often in the Old Testament, there are verses that speak not only to the situation at that moment but to the coming of the Messiah. This psalm of David, written about his misery of soul and agony of body, looked ahead to the cross of Calvary where one day Jesus would fulfill the complete meaning of these words.

As we read Psalms, we can look for these prayers that have deeper meaning. They are even useful for us to pray at times if applicable to our situation. We could not appropriate messianic prayers, but we can see ourselves often in the words and experiences and groanings and petitions of others.

There is no experience of humankind that has not already been felt by someone in some past generation.

Many of these are recorded for us in scripture. As we wait on answers to our painful circumstances, we can find expressions in the psalms that give voice to our emotions. And the comfort these passages promise becomes our own.

- Take note of psalms that resonate with your life season and needs.

- Pray psalms in moments when words are difficult to find.

- Trust God, who inspired the psalms, to be your refuge as you quote them.

• •

O God of glory and grace, You have brought to pass the fulfillment of the coming of the Messiah. Every word in Your Book is true. Guide me as I read it and study it and quote it. In Jesus' name, amen.

TOMB-SIDE PRAYERS

*Jesus wept. So the Jews said, "See how he loved him!"
But some of them said, "Could not he who opened the
eyes of the blind man also have kept this man from
dying?" Then Jesus, deeply moved again, came to the
tomb. It was a cave, and a stone lay against it. Jesus
said, "Take away the stone."... So they took away the
stone. And Jesus lifted up his eyes and said, "Father,
I thank you that you have heard me. I knew that you
always hear me, but I said this on account of the
people standing around, that they may believe that
you sent me." When he had said these things, he cried
out with a loud voice, "Lazarus, come out." The man
who had died came out, his hands and feet bound
with linen strips, and his face wrapped with a cloth.
Jesus said to them, "Unbind him, and let him go."*

JOHN 11:35–39, 41–44 ESV

. . . .

We are accustomed to prayers at a graveside. It is not
uncommon for ministers to offer prayers for comfort,
for strength, and for hope as family and friends gather
at the burial site. But it is very unusual for the minister
to speak to the dead person after the prayer.

That is exactly what Jesus, the Son of God, did.
First, He prayed to His Father: He prayed of confidence

in the presence and approval of the Father in the ministry He was performing on earth; He prayed for increased faith in those who were standing around. Then He spoke through the veil of death to the spirit world, where Lazarus was waiting in peaceful rest, and reunited him with his earthly body.

When we have the opportunity to pray around a graveside, let's. . .

- Pray in tune with the will of God and the truth of God (while never inciting anger or confusion by the way a prayer is made in times of great distress).

- Pray for the comfort of God to uphold those who have suffered loss.

• •

O God of all comfort, I am grateful for the privilege and power of prayer for others in times of suffering. Give me words to say and comfort to share. Amen.

PRAYING FOR PERSECUTORS

Now when they heard these things they were enraged, and they ground their teeth at him. But he, full of the Holy Spirit, gazed into heaven and saw the glory of God, and Jesus standing at the right hand of God. And he said, "Behold, I see the heavens opened, and the Son of Man standing at the right hand of God." But they cried out with a loud voice and stopped their ears and rushed together at him. Then they cast him out of the city and stoned him. And the witnesses laid down their garments at the feet of a young man named Saul. And as they were stoning Stephen, he called out, "Lord Jesus, receive my spirit." And falling to his knees he cried out with a loud voice, "Lord, do not hold this sin against them." And when he had said this, he fell asleep.

ACTS 7:54–60 ESV

• •

The first Christian martyr, Stephen, prayed for those who were stoning him. His prayer echoed the prayer of Jesus from the cross, "Father, forgive them."

We too are given the chance to pray for those who persecute us. Jesus taught in Matthew 5:44 (ESV), "Love your enemies and pray for those who persecute you."

It is true that most of us will not face captors with

large rocks as Stephen did, but there will be instances in our lives when we are faced with insults and cruelties, with injustices and slights. In these moments, we can choose to follow our Lord and our brother Stephen and pray for the ones who wish us harm.

- Pray that God will bless them in ways that are for their ultimate and eternal good.

- Pray that God will bless them in ways that bring Him the glory.

* *

Dear Lord Jesus, You left me the example of praying for those who intend to hurt and destroy. Please guide my words and actions as I interact with those who may persecute me in some way. Amen.

PRAYER THAT BLESSES SMALL THINGS

Now the day began to wear away, and the twelve came and said to him, "Send the crowd away to go into the surrounding villages and countryside to find lodging and get provisions, for we are here in a desolate place." But he said to them, "You give them something to eat." They said, "We have no more than five loaves and two fish—unless we are to go and buy food for all these people." For there were about five thousand men. And he said to his disciples, "Have them sit down in groups of about fifty each." And they did so, and had them all sit down. And taking the five loaves and the two fish, he looked up to heaven and said a blessing over them. Then he broke the loaves and gave them to the disciples to set before the crowd. And they all ate and were satisfied. And what was left over was picked up, twelve baskets of broken pieces.

LUKE 9:12–17 ESV

• •

There were no supermarkets or fast-food establishments in the place where Jesus was teaching. And for most people at that time, having enough food was a daily struggle. Few families could afford snacks. It was all they could do to have regular meals. Probably few of these poor people had food with them. But Jesus knew they were hungry.

There was, of course, a little boy with a lunch. At least, that's what we think it was. It could have been the day's marketing that he was bringing home for his mother. However he got it, it was all they had. And after Jesus blessed it with a prayer toward heaven, it multiplied as He gave it to the disciples to distribute. Miraculously, it kept going and going. Thank God today that. . .

- Small things become enough when they are blessed by God.

- Small things bring glory to God in a way that large things cannot.

• •

Father God, You have chosen to use small things. Help me to remember this and to pray for Your blessing on all my small offerings. Amen.

THE CASTING KINDS OF PRAYERS

Clothe yourselves, all of you, with humility toward one another, for "God opposes the proud but gives grace to the humble." Humble yourselves, therefore, under the mighty hand of God so that at the proper time he may exalt you, casting all your anxieties on him, because he cares for you. Be sober-minded; be watchful. Your adversary the devil prowls around like a roaring lion, seeking someone to devour. Resist him, firm in your faith, knowing that the same kinds of suffering are being experienced by your brotherhood throughout the world. And after you have suffered a little while, the God of all grace, who has called you to his eternal glory in Christ, will himself restore, confirm, strengthen, and establish you. To him be the dominion forever and ever. Amen.

1 PETER 5:5–11 ESV

· ·

It is easy for us to forget that we don't have to carry our burdens alone. The God we serve—this God of all grace, this eternal Christ—tells us to cast (to fling) our anxieties and heavy burdens onto Him. He cares about all that concerns us.

The attitude we should have as we pray is one of

humility, knowing that God will help only those who recognize they need it. An arrogant spirit repulses our Creator. We need to be sober-minded—that is, realizing that there are eternal consequences in our choices. We need to be watchful because the devil is always present, ready to attack and devour. And while we suffer, we can know that others are suffering too, and we can feel a camaraderie with God's family all over the world.

Praying this kind of prayer is a regular, perhaps daily, pattern. There are always new cares for us to cast. As we become more in tune with our position in Christ, we will run to Him more readily. And He will never turn us away. Consider that. . .

- The "clothing" of humility prepares us to come to God.

- The "casting" of our cares prepares us to minister to others.

* *

Lord Jesus, today I want to clothe myself and cast my cares as You have instructed me in Your Word. Give me grace to do both. Amen.

A PRAYER OF HOLY COMMISSIONING

In the year that King Uzziah died I saw the Lord sitting upon a throne, high and lifted up; and the train of his robe filled the temple. Above him stood the seraphim. . . . And one called to another and said: "Holy, holy, holy is the LORD of hosts; the whole earth is full of his glory!" . . . And I said: "Woe is me! For I am lost; for I am a man of unclean lips, and I dwell in the midst of a people of unclean lips; for my eyes have seen the King, the LORD of hosts!" Then one of the seraphim flew to me, having in his hand a burning coal that he had taken with tongs from the altar. And he touched my mouth and said: "Behold, this has touched your lips; your guilt is taken away, and your sin atoned for." And I heard the voice of the Lord saying, "Whom shall I send, and who will go for us?" Then I said, "Here I am! Send me."

ISAIAH 6:1–3, 5–8 ESV

• •

When we come into contact with God in His holiness, we are cleansed and changed, and then we are commissioned.

The prophet Isaiah had a vision of God in the temple in all His magnificent glory. This was a divine revelation since the Bible tells us that no human can see God and live. The brightness of His holiness would obliterate imperfect human beings. But God allowed Isaiah this glimpse.

Isaiah confessed that he was in need (a man of unclean lips), and the angelic being cleansed his lips with a hot coal. And then Isaiah felt the commissioning call of God to go and serve.

We will probably never have a vision like that one, but with the eyes of faith, we can glimpse the holiness of God and see our need and recognize our commission. Consider the fact that. . .

- God's holiness must cleanse us so that we reflect Him.

- God's holiness will commission us so that we can serve others.

* *

O great God, Your holiness is perfect. I ask You today to cleanse me so that my heart reflects Your purity; then send me out to do Your will. Amen.

A PRAYER FOR PURITY

Miriam and Aaron spoke against Moses because of
the Cushite woman whom he had married, for he had
married a Cushite woman. And they said, "Has the LORD
indeed spoken only through Moses? Has he not spoken
through us also?" And the LORD heard it. Now the man
Moses was very meek, more than all people who were
on the face of the earth. And suddenly the LORD said
to Moses and to Aaron and Miriam, "Come out, you
three, to the tent of meeting." And the three of them
came out.... When the cloud removed from over the
tent, behold, Miriam was leprous, like snow. And Aaron
turned toward Miriam, and behold, she was leprous.
And Aaron said to Moses, "Oh, my lord, do not punish
us because we have done foolishly and have sinned. Let
her not be as one dead, whose flesh is half eaten away
when he comes out of his mother's womb." And Moses
cried to the LORD, "O God, please heal her—please."

NUMBERS 12:1–4, 10–13 ESV

• •

In the Bible, leprosy often represents the decay of sin.
Leprosy was also a consequence God brought on some
for their disobedience. One of these instances involved
the servant Gehazi, and another involved Moses' sister,
Miriam.

Whether it was family murmuring or mean-spirited gossip, Aaron and Miriam were speaking against their younger brother, Moses. And when the cloud of God's presence moved away from the tabernacle, Miriam had an advanced stage of leprosy.

What do we do when a family member or friend speaks ill of us? Do we feel that they got what they deserved when the consequence of their mean attitude catches up to them? Or do we pray for God to lessen the burden of the punishment?

- Cry out to God for those who believe that criticism is a normal way to live.

- Cry out to God for those who are suffering because of their sin; ask for His mercy.

* *

Dear Lord, when I face those who misuse me with their words, give me a heart of compassion for them; they are miserable in the way they are living. Give me the grace of Jesus in my heart. In His name, amen.

A PRAYER OF AN EXILE

And the Lord said to Cain, Where is Abel your
brother? And he said, I do not know. Am I my brother's
keeper? And [the Lord] said, What have you done?
The voice of your brother's blood is crying to Me
from the ground. . . . Then Cain said to the Lord,
My punishment is greater than I can bear. Behold,
You have driven me out this day from the face of
the land, and from Your face I will be hidden; and I
will be a fugitive and a vagabond and a wanderer
on the earth, and whoever finds me will kill me.

GENESIS 4:9–10, 13–14 AMPC

• •

Surely the most horrible emotion is the sense of
remorse and guilt after one has willfully sinned. Cain,
the first human being to commit murder, must have
known this feeling. What a terrible moment! And
though he knew he had done wrong, he didn't turn to
God. But God went looking for him.

We do not read that Cain repented of his sin.
Instead, we read that he tried to hide it and then
became arrogant and flippant with the Lord. His
prayer to the Lord concerned himself—his safety and
future. Did he think about his parents, who would
wonder why Abel didn't come home? Did he ever go to

them and confess the wrong he had done?

In Luke 15, we read about another exile, a wanderer by choice, who left his Father's house and sinned grievously. Yet, his attitude was different; he returned asking for forgiveness. This is the kind of prayer that brings restoration.

- "And the son said to him, Father, I have sinned against heaven and in your sight; I am no longer worthy to be called your son [I no longer deserve to be recognized as a son of yours]!" (Luke 15:21 AMPC)

- Extend God's mercy to those who are in spiritual exile.

- Pray that they might speak to the Father in an attitude of returning and repenting.

. . . .

O Lord, You want to restore the exile and reclaim the prodigal. Help me be part of that redemptive work today. Amen.

A PRAYER FOR WISDOM

In Gibeon the LORD appeared to Solomon in a dream by night: and God said, Ask what I shall give thee. And Solomon said, . . .O LORD my God, thou hast made thy servant king instead of David my father: and I am but a little child: I know not how to go out or come in. And thy servant is in the midst of thy people which thou hast chosen, a great people, that cannot be numbered nor counted for multitude. Give therefore thy servant an understanding heart to judge thy people, that I may discern between good and bad: for who is able to judge this thy so great a people? And the speech pleased the LORD, that Solomon had asked this thing.

1 KINGS 3:5–10 KJV

• •

The Bible tells us that Solomon was the wisest man who ever lived. How did he become so wise? His wisdom was a direct gift from God.

Solomon had a humble spirit. He saw himself as a little child in ways of kingly leadership, and he knew that he needed help. When God asked him for a request, Solomon had one ready. He wanted to be able to judge the people fairly and to discern between right and wrong so that God's people might be aptly led. God was pleased with this request.

Solomon's gift was unusual. That's the reason we know about it. God chose to put it in the Bible because it was something out of the ordinary. But even today, the Word of God promises that we can have wisdom for daily living if we ask "If any of you lacks wisdom, let him ask of God, who gives to all liberally and without reproach, and it will be given to him" (James 1:5 NKJV).

We are not earthly royalty; we do not judge or rule. But we need wisdom in our daily lives. God tells us to ask.

- Pray for wisdom to distinguish between right and wrong.

- Pray for discernment in your dealings with others.

* *

Dear Father in heaven, give me divine wisdom this day as I do my best to follow Your will and bring glory to Jesus. I ask it in His name. Amen.

SCRIPTURE INDEX

OLD TESTAMENT

NEW TESTAMENT

ABOUT THE AUTHOR

Valorie Quesenberry is a pastor's wife, mother, grand-mother, musician, adjunct professor, and writer. She periodically contributes devotional writings to a Christian literature provider. Her first book released April 2010.